School Genetics
A Blueprint for Saving Public Schools

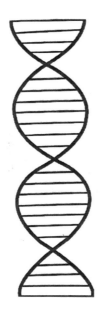

Dr. Craig Lockhart, NBCT

"School Genetics: A Blueprint for Saving Public Schools" Copyright © 2015 by Dr. Craig Lockhart

First Asta Publications, LLC paperback edition

All rights reserved. No part of this publication may be reproduced, stored in a retrieval system, or transmitted in any form or by any means without the prior permission of the publisher, except for brief quotations in reviews or articles.

ISBN: 978-1-934947-93-7

Cover Designed by: Brittany Goss

Printed in the United States of America

*Dedicated to the children, families, and communities
who depend on public education
to give them a brighter future.*

TABLE OF CONTENTS

Introduction- Read This First!... 1

Building Background Knowledge:
A Tale of Two Schools.. 5

Lesson 1: School Genetics 11

Lesson 2: It Starts (and Ends) with the Leader..................... 20

Lesson 3: Good Teachers- Essential Building Blocks
For Good Schools... 40

Lesson 4: Professional Learning Communities....................... 58

Lesson 5: Leadership is a Team Sport..................................... 65

Lesson 6: Taylor County Upper Elementary:
The Journey from Worst to First 75

Lesson 7: Newton High School-
Rams Rise!... 95

Lesson 8: Discipline 99

Conclusion... 121

INTRODUCTION- READ THIS FIRST!

This book is all about the fight to save public education. Public confidence in the country's ability to provide a quality, free, and appropriate education appears to have eroded severely due to political agendas, media sensationalism, Internet opinions, and general perceptions that the public school system is beyond saving. As of 2015, media and political agendas would make one think that there are only two voices that are heard regarding public education: those who wish to see it burn, and those who say nothing at all. I would like to believe that many, many people appreciate the public education system, but we do not hear them. There are strong, experienced champions of public education, but they are seemingly so few in number that their voices remain small.

I write this book today to argue that the persecution of public education is wrong and largely unjustified. Our public schools are an integral part of the American Dream, and public schools remain very capable of educating our children. I have served as a teacher, administrator, principal, and assistant/deputy superintendent, and I am tired of the public beating and torturing of one of the most enduring institutions in our society: public education. Since the creation of the United States Constitution, education has been a property right for American citizens. It is a liberty that every American is entitled to receive. It has changed significantly over the years, but it constantly produces individuals who have become our civil servants, doctors, lawyers, engineers, great thinkers, and our world leaders. Education matters, and public education is the lifeblood for our economy and communities. The time has come to dispel myths and share our successes.

Are some schools better than others? Absolutely. In every field, there are individuals and organizations that function at higher qualities than others. There are churches that are better, police forces that are better, doctors who are better, cleaning services that are better, cars that are better, hamburgers that are better, malls that are better, athletes who are better, and the list goes on and on. Schools, however, take a lashing unlike other institutions or products. One reason is because those who work inside schools (teachers, school officials, etc.) typically do not "fight back." Check the local newspapers and news channels to confirm this. When a teacher makes a mistake that ends up in the news, we rarely hear the teacher's side of the story. Even in collective bargaining states where teachers have a bit more negotiating strength, public education is often scorned, and the people who serve in them are labeled as people who get summer vacations and the weekends off. In fact, many people take educators for granted and view schools as a babysitting service. If you require evidence to support that last statement, read social media reactions when school is unexpectedly closed for a day.

School Genetics: A Blueprint for Saving Public Education is not a book solely about theory or research. This book is driven by proven experience grounded in real situations, real life, and in real time. All of the best practices found in this book have underpinnings based in research and theory, but this book is designed to be user-friendly and practical. Educators are pretty familiar with "best practices" and what research says about effective teaching and learning, but for some reason, a lot of that research-based practice does not surface in many classrooms. Why? Many schools recognize the "what" (theory), but practitioners often grapple with the "how" (practice). Practical proven experience gets work done, and many educators simply cannot translate theory into best practice. Hopefully, readers will identify with some of the stories and techniques shared in this book. To the reader, *School Genetics: A Blueprint for Saving Public Schools* will read like a speech, editorial, plea, blog, sermon, and journal at times, but all of that is intentional so that you can experience some of what happens in the real world of education. This is a conversation among colleagues. It is my sincere hope that these lessons either shed light on new innovations or at least affirm the right things that educators are doing in schools. This book looks at some hard topics so that we can adequately address the right issues, but it is also designed to add a blend of humor in a field that so desperately needs to be able to enjoy a laugh sometimes.

How do you read this book? First, please know the thoughts contained are based on my personal journey at two schools that would be classified as "at-risk" which were able to see sustained success academically. The thoughts here are my personal experiences not endorsed by any school system. The work you will see in this book is based on the hard work of many teachers, staff, students, and families. Maybe

School Genetics: A Blueprint for Saving Public Schools

I did nothing. I just happened to be in the right place, at the right time with the right people. While I was in the right place, I chose to record the journeys so that the educational community could learn about our school's successes as well as learn from our failures.

This book should be read and studied based upon the school improvement strategies that are deemed necessary for that particular school. Therefore, the book is broken into lessons: some of the lessons are lengthier than others, but all play a role in school improvement. A short lesson is short only because the answer is pretty straightforward and direct. Other lessons may be longer because the full aspect of the concept may require much more discussion and thought.

This is a call to action for the support of public education. Our schools are a direct reflection of the communities they serve. To give up on our schools is to give up on the people who live in that area, which means we are giving up on fellow human beings. We are better than that. The community makeup, or "genetic code," can be cracked when it comes to the climate and operation of our schools, and this can be done when our schools have the right support and leadership. It is my sincere hope that this book offers some aid in the fight to restore public education to the level of prominence and importance that it so richly deserves.

BUILDING BACKGROUND KNOWLEDGE: A TALE OF TWO SCHOOLS

The practices and experiences described in this book are based on two actual journeys that I experienced in two entirely different school settings. There were good days, and there were an awful lot of mistakes. Both journeys changed my life forever, and at a minimum, hopefully, someone will read this book and avoid the pitfalls that I did.

The first experience was when I served as principal of Taylor County Upper Elementary School in Butler, Georgia. The year was 2004. This was a reconfigured school that was developed after grades Kindergarten, first, and second were moved to another site. The resulting school combined grades Prekindergarten, three, four, five, and six. In addition, an elementary version of a psycho-educational program was also housed there--students in this program reported to Taylor County Upper Elementary from three partnering school districts.

The Taylor County School System at that time served approximately 1,700 students in grades Kindergarten through twelve. This rural school system had many of the typical challenges small school systems face: limited funding, professional learning that did not always resonate with staff members, and an overreliance on traditional teaching methods. The school itself housed approximately 600 students, thus making it the largest populated school in the system at the time. Over 70% of the students received free and/or reduced lunch, and one out of every seven students had been labeled as being in need of some form of special educational services.

When I was appointed to the new building, I also inherited a label that remained with it. Under the No Child Left Behind Act (NCLB) of 2001, the school had an Adequate Yearly Progress (AYP) designation of being in Needs Improvement Four (NI-4) status. A school that did not meet all of the prescribed state benchmarks was dubbed as "having not made AYP," and would then enter a number of years of needs improvement status. Thus, my first appointment as a principal was at a school that was already in dire straits based on the accountability model of the day.

During my first two years there, I thought I could single-handedly fix the problems at the school. I had actually attended school in the very same building as a child and had graduated from this school system. This is a place I love dearly, and I was dedicated to uplifting the children and people in that community. My vision was noble, but narrow. I was overly confident that I could get the job done alone. After all, I had served as a teacher and administrator in the very progressive metropolitan DeKalb County School System, so I felt more than equipped to handle this small elementary school of less than 600 students. At that time, I did not consciously use any of the practices that will be described in this book. So what was the result? After two additional years of not making Adequate Yearly Progress, I led the school to earning an NI-6 designation. Despite the fact that our students were in the newspaper weekly for doing many great things, we were in a bad situation where federal and state legislations were concerned. To add insult to injury, a report from the Georgia Department of Education showed that only one elementary school in the entire state had reached the NI-6 designation that year, making my beloved little school, by AYP standards alone, the "worst elementary school in the state of Georgia." See the chart on the next page.

School Genetics: A Blueprint for Saving Public Schools

Georgia Department of Education
2004 - 2005 Needs Improvement - By the Numbers

System Level Information

Number of Systems that Made AYP = 83

Number of Systems that Did Not Make AYP = 100

Number of Systems that are required to have a System Improvement Plan = 9

School Level Information

	Elementary	Middle	High	Other	Total
Number of Schools that Met AYP	1200	244	223	3	1670
Number of Schools that Did Not Meet AYP	52	181	131	6	370
Total	1252	425	354	9	2040

	Elementary	Middle	High	Other	Total
Number of Distinguished Schools	990	52	64	1	1107

	Elementary	Middle	High	Other	Total
NI Years = 1 (Choice)	5	76	63	3	147
NI Years = 2 (Supplemental Educational Services)	9	48	36	0	93
NI Years = 3 (Identified for Corrective Action)	4	20	3	2	29
NI Years = 4 (Identified for Restructuring)	9	9	1	0	19
NI Years = 5 (Implementation of Restructuring Plan)	4	14	0	0	18
NI Years = 6 (Implementation of Restructuring Plan Yr 2)	1	22	1	0	24
NI Years = 7 (See Note 1)	0	12	2	0	14
NI Years = 8	0	9	1	0	10
Total	32	210	107	5	354

Note 1. All schools in Needs Improvement Year 7 or higher must implement Year 6 consequences in the 2005-2006 school year.

School Genetics: A Blueprint for Saving Public Schools

The number "1" listed on the chart was us. It was I. I remember sitting in my office and seeing that report. My world was caving in on me. I grieved for my good-hearted staff. I felt the disappointment of my beloved community. I felt sorry for my students and their families. I was also very angry. They did not deserve this designation. I did not know if I had what it took to move forward, but I had to keep fighting for our students and staff.

I will share more of Taylor County Upper Elementary School's fate later. Let's fast forward to the more recent past. In September 2010, I was named principal of Newton High School in Covington, Georgia. At the time, the Newton County School System served approximately 19,000 students in a suburban community that in 2008 was named one of the fastest growing communities in the nation. A new superintendent arrived in the county with a strong instructional background and over 20 years of experience as a superintendent. The school system was poised for academic success despite the severe economic challenges it would have to face. For many years, the school was the only high school in the school system. The existing Newton High School opened in 1974, and Newton High was to be moved to a brand new facility in 2013. At one time, the school housed over 3,000 students in grades nine through twelve. Other school openings dropped its enrollment to approximately 1,800 students. At the time of my arrival, the free and/or reduced lunch population had swelled to over 70%. The school served more special needs students than the other two high schools in the county. A demographic shift occurred in the mid-2000s in which the population changed to over 80% African-American students, a stark contrast to the school's demographics at the turn of the millennium. The teachers had remained pretty much the same faculty, but the clientele was very different. A gang culture became more prevalent, and traditional teaching practices that once satisfied the norm were no longer as engaging. The school had made AYP hit or miss over the past eight years, and the school was struggling with finding its new identity. Overnight, a school community possessing a rural mindset had been placed in a world of urban issues. Leadership had changed rapidly over the past few years, and I was coming in as the second African-American principal in the school's history. There was division between "Old" Newton High and "New" Newton High educators, between black and white staff, between new and veteran teachers, and between clashing philosophies on how to best educate students who were totally different from those of years past.

LESSON 1

SCHOOL GENETICS

The background of the aforementioned schools is important because if one is to focus on improving schools, one must first understand the idea of **school genetics**. School genetics is the makeup of the school. The concept of school genetics can be related to human genetics. For the purpose of this lesson, we will divide school genetics into two categories: Appearance and Health. *School Appearance* is what the public can easily see and/or observe at a school. Examples of appearance include the physical state and cleanliness of the building and grounds, media reports, disciplinary issues, etc. *School Health* involves what is "inside the school" -quality of teaching and learning, strong professionally developed practices, strategic planning and operations, school pride, and school climate. School Genetics can be categorized into four categories:

> Category A- Good Appearance/Good Health
> Category B- Good Appearance/Bad Health
> Category C- Bad Appearance/Good Health
> Category D- Bad Appearance/Bad Health

One way to visualize the four categories is with a school genetics version of a Punnett Square. A Punnett Square is a diagram that allows us to predict various types of genetic traits an offspring may exhibit. An example of a

School Genetics: A Blueprint for Saving Public Schools

Punnett Square demonstrating four categories of schools as outlined on the previous page can be found below:

	Good Appearance	Bad Appearance
Good Health	**A** Good Appearance/ Good Health	**B** Bad Appearance/ Good Health
Bad Health	**C** Good Appearance/ Bad Health	**D** Bad Appearance/ Bad Health

The "good" and "bad" terms are used in a very broad general context. In fact, the very use of the words "good" and "bad" is merely an oversimplification of the conditions being described. For example, a school with a "Bad Appearance" may be in a very old building, but may have absolutely no discipline issues.

Which Type is Your School?

Type A- Good Appearance/Good Health

The first level of school genetics is Category A. Some humans

School Genetics: A Blueprint for Saving Public Schools

have really good genes. These people look great, do not have to exercise or diet much, are healthy, have beautiful eyes, skin, hair, etc. They do not have to do much in order to take care of their bodies. Their outward appearance and overall health is good. Schools with similar genetics are able to run almost without a principal. Students come to the school ready to learn. Teachers are committed to the work, understand their role in the education process, and take responsibility for the orderly operation and learning within the school. The building is clean, and discipline issues are virtually non-existent. School pride is abundant among the students, faculty, parents, and community. This is a utopic experience reserved by only a few schools.

Type B- Bad Appearance/Good Health

Category B is a school that may be a bit older, but practices within are solid. These schools may not be in the newest facilities, but the culture is one of high expectations and a caring spirit. In many cases, these schools are community-based schools that are adored by the people in the neighborhoods. Many of the students who go to these schools have had family members attend them for generations, and the school is a staple of the community. Even when there are unpleasant issues that happen at these schools, the community remains largely supportive of the institution. As you can see, the use of the word "bad" really does not indicate poor quality; it merely shows that the outward appearance does not rise to the level of "good," or "new." In fact, thorough, consistent cleaning and/or building renovations will quickly move this type of school from a Type B to

School Genetics: A Blueprint for Saving Public Schools

Type A.

Type C- Good Appearance/Bad Health

Category C is comparable to the person that looks good on the outside but is not healthy on the inside. Signs of this type of school are those that have generally been able to meet No Child Left Behind goals but may not be progressive enough to overcome increasing assessment benchmarks without effort. Staff members often do not believe that more rigorous assessments are coming, and they teach "to the middle" of their students' proficiency levels. Teachers in these schools think they are doing a good job but do not realize that they are unintentionally communicating low expectations by not sufficiently challenging their students. One of the main issues for Category C schools is that they may be in trouble, but they do not know it yet.

Type D- Bad Appearance/Bad Health

The final type of school genetics is the school whose makeup causes it to look bad both inside and out. This is Category D, or the "failing schools" class. The buildings are usually older, but discipline issues are so prevalent that even a new building loses its luster in the wake of the behavioral problems. Academically, these schools perform at low levels in comparison to their peers. Many teachers in these settings are often at such a point of frustration that strategy and collaboration have given away to cynicism and fear. If one were to listen to conversations in the general community, many people would erroneously be led to believe that the

School Genetics: A Blueprint for Saving Public Schools

majority of public schools are Category D Schools.

Is the Public Right?

All too often, members of the public confuse student behavior with the quality of the school itself. These citizens seem to carry a belief that the teachers and school leaders are the biggest problem in these schools. The further removed these same citizens are from the school, the more it appears their opinions have been solidified. These citizens live in a luxury of ignorance. Contrary to belief, teachers do not teach profanity in English class. They do not teach how to make drugs in science; they do not teach gambling in math. These teachers do not teach students how to fight in physical education, nor do they teach gang affiliation in social studies. Educators in these schools work with the raw product (students) that comes through the doors each day. Despite this truth, one of the first recommendations in a school takeover model includes the removal of the teaching staff and its leaders. I challenge the policy makers, thinkers, and the greater citizenry to visit these schools to learn more about them before making unfounded assumptions about the quality of the staff in the school as well as the generalizing of the character of all of the children within a "failing" school. The results would be surprising.

There are a few observations to be taken from the concept of school genetics. First, if the Appearance of the school looks good, the majority of the public will tolerate it regardless of the Health. Public perception is intangible, but it is very real. In fact, this is the heart of the concept of a "Good School." I have asked people over the years, "What is a good school?", and many people struggle or hesitate with answering that question. Some people think that a good school is one that is selective in its entrance criteria or one that is faith-based; the concept of a good school in this discussion focuses on our traditional public schools. In a traditionally-run public school, good schools are often described as schools that demonstrate high levels of order. "Good schools" may be in older buildings, but there is a strong sense of security and order present. *Make no mistake about it: before there can be teaching and learning, there must be safety and order.* As we all know, we cannot prepare or prevent every issue that happens in schools, but parents want to generally assume and know that their children will return home in the evening in the same or better condition than when they left them in the morning. This means exposing children to other children whose parents also explicitly value safe and orderly environments. Safe schools often equate to "good" schools, and well-meaning parents insist that their children attend good schools. That is a reasonable request.

Another note in the school genetics model is that it takes motivated, strategic, and passionate leaders and teachers to move the school to a better level of performance. This is a critical statement because with the right work taking place, schools can be improved or "fixed", just as appearance and health can be improved to some degree with the right elements of exercise, diet, and care. This is where the comparison between school genetics and human genetics becomes crucial: we cannot change our genetic structure easily. The building blocks of genes are found within DNA. The "DNA" of our schools consists of our student clientele, teacher effectiveness, and leadership.

In regards to students, we can change buildings, leaders, teachers and staff members, but we have no control over the product that walks in and out of the doors each day. Students come to us with wide ranges of experiences, emotions, expectations, socioeconomic conditions, and cultural beliefs that shape their behavior and their perception of learning.

Another part of the school's DNA is the ability and traits of the teacher. If the teacher 1) cannot relate to students, 2) does not hold students to high expectations, and/or 3) is not passionate about teaching and learning, then students from at-risk backgrounds are less likely to receive them well. When students go home each afternoon and parents ask them about their day, the child's answer often gives the parent an impression of the school. If the teacher is caring and the child says this to parents in his or her own unique way, then the parents are reassured and are more likely to support the school.

Students and teachers shape the genetic makeup of the school. Unless we perform "school plastic surgery" by rezoning populations, terminating mediocre staff without regard to tenure rights, or creating socially engineered schools that allow us to select students and remove the poor performers without regard to due process rights, we must educate the children who walk into our classrooms with the resources we have been provided. The fact that public schools are obligated to teach all who enter the buildings makes it completely different from any other business: the "raw material" that schools work with has a *free will* and can choose to accept or reject the teachings. Schools cannot be compared to the business world. Schools are different from the business world, and the public must recognize this fact. The DNA of the school influences our genetic appearance and health. Since *all* children must be educated, "school plastic surgery" alone will not fix social and academic issues in our schools. Our "genes" are our genes. Teachers and students will both do what comes naturally to them. As a popular saying goes, "it is what it is."

So What Do We Do?

Even though our genes are set, we can have great influence over them through the engagement of activities designed to improve Appearance and Health. As humans, we are genetically predisposed to certain conditions and/or illnesses. With proper care, however, we can improve our appearance and health by engaging in certain practices. The same practices can be applied to fixing schools in the following ways:

Diet and Exercise--The "diet" is what the school actually takes into its building. Just as we ingest food, the diet of the school is what materials we choose to absorb in order to survive. Dietary items include the curriculum, adopted instructional practices, and appropriate professional learning. Exercise refers to the "what" we actually do to affect change. Exercise includes teaching by using best practices, monitoring of effective practices, and modification of ineffective practices when observed. Diet and exercise are grouped together because they are interdependent and positively or negatively influence the other.

Another important component of improving school genetics is rest. "Rest" in this context means taking time to celebrate accomplishments. This impacts the school culture. Too often, our schools have become oppressive testing factories in which teacher morale is low and the threat of a school takeover is high. Celebrations must occur both large and small to improve schools.

A critical need in improving school genetics is medical support. When a person goes to the doctor, they receive a diagnosis on their current status of health. In schools, we have high-stakes standardized yearly assessments that tell us about our condition. Schools must assess students regularly to track growth and development. Just as with a health diagnosis, schools are able to determine if they need to stay on the current track, make modifications, or even prepare for full-blown surgery.

I shared that the DNA of a school consists of the students, teachers, and the leaders. The next lesson looks in depth at the role of the principal in school improvement. So goes the principal, so goes the school.

LESSON 2

IT STARTS (AND ENDS) WITH THE LEADER

If one wishes to fix a school, then proactive, deliberate actions must take place. The first step involves the leader and the adults surrounding that leader. Researchers have proven undeniably that the major contributor to student achievement is the teacher. I would also state that another major contributor to school improvement is the principal. The principal's role is so important to the overall improvement of the school that significant time must be spent discussing this position.

The principal is the beginning and the end of school improvement. He or she is the gatekeeper to all things in the school. Federal mandates, state rules, district requirements, and community requests all are interpreted and funneled through the school by the principal.

Many teachers aspire to become a principal. In the business of education, promotions are often difficult to come by. There are far too many teachers and only a handful of administrative positions. People who are named as administrators are not always internal candidates. Many teachers see administrative jobs as a way to escape the classroom, not realizing that the work of an administrator is often more time-consuming and very complex. I have known many educators who view the principalship in an idealist state. Many think that to be a principal is to go around to dinner parties or social gatherings and proclaim, "I am the principal!" The reality is that there is very little that is glamorous about being a principal.

Politics? But I was Hired to Be the Principal!

The principalship has always been riddled with politics. Principals are local celebrities in their communities, especially at the high school level. How principals handle discipline issues with certain children and how principals show support for various teachers are prime examples of how principals are judged and perceived as leaders. These intricate problems were tough to deal with in decades prior to the 2000s, but in the age of accountability and the expansion of the Internet, the weight of being a principal magnified to unprecedented levels. The No Child Left Behind Act of 2001 stated that schools and districts had to demonstrate measured improvement on a variety of academic benchmarks in order to be considered as good, successful schools. Failure to do so had a variety of consequences, which included, but was not limited to: the threat of state takeovers of schools, public shame, increased advocacy for charter and other non-public school options, and termination of faculty members, most notably the principal. For the first time, the principal's career was directly tied to the performance of students. In many cases, this was a good thing because schools legitimately rose to the occasion. In other cases, people have been pressured and even intimidated into producing good results, and they become desperate and resort to changing student test

School Genetics: A Blueprint for Saving Public Schools

answers in attempts to keep their jobs.

Dealing with human resources is also a politically slippery slope. Some faculty members are mediocre at best, and terminating them would be the most ideal solution. These same mediocre staff members, however, are often connected by blood or some other relationship to persons who have great influence on the work of the school and/or system. Even in metropolitan districts, many principals find that they must tread carefully in these all-too-real situations. A casual outsider may quickly say that the principal must fire such employees, but the reality is often far from that idealistic response. Just the same, some action must be taken. It is incumbent upon principals, at a minimum, to place mediocre persons in places where they can do the least amount of damage to the instructional program as possible. In the long term, principals must have the courage and tenacity to support, monitor, and document teachers, so that they can improvem or exit.

Staff selection is critical, so superintendents and boards of education must make the right decisions when recruiting, selecting, hiring, promoting, demoting, and terminating staff. Staff hired solely for emotional or political reasons often hinder the school improvement process when the persons selected are not the best fit for the job. Often, the most contentious issues that divide and/or plague board members and superintendents are personnel issues. While the superintendent is charged with recommending the hiring, transferring, promoting, demoting, or non-renewing of staff, the board of education must approve such recommendations. This becomes very sticky when there are outside relationships that impact such decisions. Many board members, superintendents, and school leaders have relationships with staff outside of work, such as family ties, church affiliations, friendships, favors owed, racial sentiments, and a host of other reasons. These bonds can often cloud judgment, and schools are compromised when emotions or ulterior motives win the day. The superintendent and principal must focus on placing the best people in the right positions, and the board must support these efforts when the data clearly shows that the best people are being selected for positions. Schools will never move forward if we keep hiring and retaining mediocre staff members. Evidence must trump emotions every time in the human resources business. In other words, *it's personnel, not personal.*

The rise of social media also makes principals (and other school system leaders) targets of ridicule and contempt. For decades, principals have often been despised for their work. Parents of disciplined children are often not supportive, and they spread their contempt to anyone willing to listen. Teachers are also sometimes critical and wary of principals, and that is not always without reason. That disdain for many principals has intensified through the use of social media. Teacher, principal, and school ranking sites are used to further spread the perceived weaknesses of school employees, and these opinions are often taken as the gospel. Anonymous bloggers are able to warp opinions to the point that it becomes the truth to the untrained mind.

School Genetics: A Blueprint for Saving Public Schools

The greatest challenge of a leader at any level is that there are people who, when driven by their desperation and fear, are capable of exacting great evil against the leader. This evil manifests in many forms: insubordination, sabotage, character assassination, intense arguments, fights, and even death threats. This is nothing new; leaders in all career fields have always been the target of opposing forces. The challenge for a school leader is to be willing to stand against those who may not fully understand the pathway to obtaining a high-quality education. Leaders must remember that they are often judged by how they handle crises, and their legacies depend upon those very actions.

The principalship is a heavy burden, and the people in those roles must be mentally, emotionally, and physically prepared to deal with the stresses that accompany the position. There is no crying in the principalship. There is very little that is glamorous about serving as a principal. In fact, many principals fall in love with their school and their teaching staff only to find that they have very little support within their own schools. Aspiring leaders must take time to truly understand themselves and their ability to cope with highly stressful situations before they opt to choose this career path. It is not for the faint of heart.

The Right Fit For the School

Principals must be good fits for the schools they are appointed to lead. There must be a "genetic compatibility" between the principal and the school. It bears repeating: so goes the principal, so goes the school. The principal and the school are ONE and should be viewed interchangeably.

School Genetics: A Blueprint for Saving Public Schools

Therefore, the principal and school must be directly in sync with one another. For instance, a principal with years of experience in a tough, inner-city school may not be the best fit for a Category A school. Likewise, a principal who never had to confront gang issues may not fare well in a Category D school. Some leaders are only built for elementary settings, whereas others will only work at middle or high school. Some principals are "peacetime leaders." Peacetime principals are community builders who perform well in schools that do not have academic or disciplinary struggles. They know how to balance the politics that are often more prevalent due to the usually higher socioeconomic status for the families they serve. Other principals are "wartime principals." Wartime principals are not hired to make friends. They must focus only on the tough task of establishing order and making student achievement gains under stressed conditions. Both types of principals are needed to serve their respective clienteles. I am of the belief that few persons exist who can be successful in all four Categories of schools.

Do race and/or gender matter in the selection of the right principal for a school? Race, gender, age, experience, and popularity all play roles in the success of principals, and both internal school and external public communities are quite cognizant of that assertion even if they do not say so aloud. I have seen persons whose skill set have allowed for them to overcome community perceptions as to whether or not the person is the right fit. My personal experience is that if the principal loves that school and possesses certain professional traits needed to improve schools, then the love and skill of the leader are far more important than skin color, gender, or any other condition that may be considered for principal assignment. Ideally, leaders and all school staff for that matter, should be hired based on the skills they bring to the organization. We must attempt to balance the need to be sensitive and representative of the school's clientele with the need to get the right work done effectively. Hiring anyone solely to meet racial or gender quotas does not always guarantee success. Performance matters. School systems should adopt the mantra, "Hire the right principal for the right principle."

The Genetic Makeup of the Principal

The first trait that a principal must possess is a high emotional intelligence. The old saying is true: it is lonely at the top. In a school, there is only one principal. She or he is the beginning and the end. When an intruder enters the school, the principal, in theory, is the first line of defense. If the building is on fire, the principal, in theory, is the last one out to make sure everyone else is safe. Every decision made in that school belongs to the principal, whether she made that decision or not, whether she is even aware that a decision has been made. The principal's name is often used as leverage in many situations unbeknownst to the principal. No one knows what it feels like to be in the "big chair" at a school until they are sitting in it. Principals often have trusted confidantes, but even the confidantes cannot know, or even understand, everything. Again, this is not a job for the squeamish or faint of heart. Every move a principal makes is subject to scrutiny and criticism. The principal must have the emotional strength to withstand the numerous obstacles that she will be faced with daily.

In addition to possessing high emotional intelligence, a principal must be careful not to get too emotionally invested in his teachers. This is a common problem. When we become too emotionally invested in our teachers, we tend to overlook poor performance or bad decisions that teachers make. Principals often view teachers as family over a period of time, given the amount of time they spend together. One must be mindful that in a family, good parents address and even discipline children when disobedience or mistakes occur. A friend is willing to tell you an inconvenient truth; an enemy will allow you to keep making the same mistake until it leads to your downfall. A principal must show care and concern for his staff but balance this love by being able to clearly identify teacher deficiencies or issues and confront those behaviors expeditiously.

The principal must be able to cast a vision. Where does the principal want the school to be academically at the end of the school year? What do we want the school to look like at the end of the year? What will a child who completes the grade span at your school be able to do when he or she moves to the next level? What will the community view as the core values, persona, and legacy of the school in five years, ten years, or more? The vision sets the path to the answer of the aforementioned questions. This is more difficult than it sounds for many leaders. The principal, in alignment with the school district, casts a vision about what is expected to occur in the school. Oftentimes, teachers can be heard saying that they are not sure of their leader's vision.

School Genetics: A Blueprint for Saving Public Schools

Some teachers do not believe the leader will hold his word about his vision and thus adopt the "this too shall pass" mentality. The leader must be very intentional and deliberate in setting the vision for the school. The vision must be clear and realistic. Every person in the building should be familiar with the vision, and the leader would be wise to reiterate the vision frequently to keep it fresh and at the center of the school work. One method for ensuring that the vision is the core business in the school is to establish common expectations for the school. Common expectations are agreed upon non-negotiable practices/standards that staff and leaders develop in order to realize the vision of the school. A set of common expectations, also known as non-negotiable goals, helps faculty and staff remain focused on the few critical duties that each educator needs to focus on. Setting common expectations reminds staff what is of utmost importance among the hundreds of different tasks and situations that arise during a school day. It is critical that the common expectations are discussed and agreed upon by the school leadership team and preferably, by the entire faculty. Having staff members help build and endorse the common expectations of the school encourages ownership and a stronger agreement among the staff. On pages 29-31 you will find common instructional expectations used by staff at Taylor Upper Elementary School and Newton High School. In addition, a third set of common expectations dedicated to organizational goals was created and supported by the staff at Newton High. These expectations were printed and placed in every teacher's classroom and served as the standard for how business was to be run in these institutions.

School Genetics: A Blueprint for Saving Public Schools

Taylor County Upper Elementary Common Expectations 2008-2009

All teachers in TCUES will be held to the following common expectations:

I. Maintain high expectations for all students and demand high standards of work at all times.
II. Be able to identify targeted students that we teach and place them in tiers of instruction.
III. Adhere to a workshop format that consists of an opening, work period, and closing that has a research base and has been agreed upon by each department at each grade level.
IV. Implement the TCUES Response-To -Intervention plan as the process for using formative assessments properly for each student. Action plans must be developed for each child based on their assessment performances.
V. Artifacts must be posted in the classrooms. Common artifacts include: standards that are clearly posted, appropriate student work pieces, appropriate teacher commentaries, and up-to-date 25 Books Campaign charts.
VI. Teachers must track the 25 Books progress of their students and effectively respond when students are not meeting their quarterly reading goals.
VII. The GPS frameworks will guide our instruction.

School Genetics: A Blueprint for Saving Public Schools

Newton High School
Common Instructional Expectations
2012-2013

All faculty/staff in NHS will be held to the following common instructional expectations:

I. Maintain high expectations for all students and demand high standards of work at all times.
II. Implement state & locally adopted curriculum with fidelity.
III. Use research based instructional strategies, background knowledge techniques, and technology integration to engage students in their learning.
IV. Assess students' mastery of content frequently, and analyze this data to modify instruction as needed. Provide interventions when students need extra support.
V. Participate in professional learning communities as designed by the school/system, and use these practices in regular instruction.

School Genetics: A Blueprint for Saving Public Schools

Newton High School
Common Organizational Expectations
2012-2013

All faculty/staff in NHS will be held to the following common organizational expectations:

I. Communicate and demonstrate positive interpersonal skills while interacting with students, parents, other teachers, administrators, and other school personnel.
II. Report to work and duty assignments on time and display regular attendance.
III. Adhere to school and local system procedures and rules.
IV. Demonstrate positive personal conduct, including manner of attire, while in the performance of school duties.

School Genetics: A Blueprint for Saving Public Schools

The next trait that a principal must possess is that he must be the instructional leader of the school. Decades ago, the principal did not need to have strong instructional knowledge to be successful. In the Age of Accountability, it is an absolute necessity for a principal to understand how the best instructional practices positively influence student achievement. A strong instructional leader must be able to go into any classroom, any grade, any subject matter, and be able to identify the best instructional practices. The instructional leader must be able to look at curriculum guides and understand what he is viewing. Fortunately, this is a skill that can be learned by a principal who is willing to dedicate himself to studying the best practices. In addition to being knowledgeable of the best instructional practices, the principal must communicate more to the faculty, students, and parents. This is the core of the vision that the principal must set if he is focused on school improvement. If the principal is not the recognized instructional leader who advocates proactively for the best teaching and learning, then school improvement is dead at the door.

The principal must be a change agent. Educational reforms have been a part of the educational landscape since the concept of of formal education came into existence. We saw several reforms come about in the 21st Century as America responded to various changes around the world. When NCLB came along in the early 2000s, the reforms accelerated at an unusual pace. In the state of Georgia, for example, curriculum evolved from the Quality Core Curriculum, to the Georgia Performance Standards, to the Common Core Georgia Performance Standards in less than a decade. There are students who have been educated through three curricular formats during their K-12 experience. Other changes, such as new teacher evaluation methods and assessment requirements, also keep schools and districts trying to balance what is essential to teaching and learning and meeting accountability benchmarks. A savvy principal must be able to navigate the ever changing forces while keeping teachers calm and focused.

Principals must not only demonstrate the skill to turn around a school, but they must also possess the *will* to do so. Skills can be taught, sharpened, and honed through professional learning, research, and experience. Will, however, is something that one must possess in his or her mental toolbox. Will is the ability to take best practices and see them through to completion. Many times, educators learn of great things through presentations, books, and consultants, but the momentum to start the process and see it through eventually fades. Principals become bogged down in day-to-day management issues and sometimes forget the "big picture." When this happens, the goal to set about turning around a school becomes too big and far-fetched, and what seemed to be a noble endeavor becomes nothing more than the equivalent of a failed New Year's resolution. Will manifests itself as "follow through," and follow through garners respect. Follow through by the principal creates a "says-what-he-means-and means-what-he-says" culture. You can teach skill, but you must exhibit will.

I would strongly argue that the most effective principals must possess a passion for the work that exudes itself in the person's charisma, enthusiasm, and willingness to get the right work done. A principal that possesses this type of energy is able to create a positive environment amongst stakeholders that is both contagious and infectious. The principal must be able to sell his brand to teachers, students, and parents so that they are willing to follow. In high-poverty schools, hope is often scarce. Therefore, the principal must be able to generate healthy energy and confidence from stakeholders in order to get them to forget about the barriers to learning and focus on the business at hand.

The principal must be a strategist. I have observed that many principals know WHAT needs to be done, but they struggle with the HOW. As a strategist, the principal must always work on maintaining FOCUS in areas of student achievement, more effective teaching, and enhanced school improvement. The only way to achieve and maintain this level of focus is to be strategic. She must have a plan and several contingency plans in place. Teachers will come and go, so the principal must have a plan in place to ensure the sustainability of school improvement initiatives. More details about developing strategy will be explored as we review action planning in Lesson 5.

The principal must be a provocateur. The principal must be willing to ask the tough questions and expose the proverbial elephant in the room. For too long, educators and the community have been unwilling to publicly state and confront disparities among racial lines that have led to achievement gaps between white students and children of color. Despite our collective intellect, we choose not to use our wisdom and experience to maturely discuss matters of student achievement that cross color lines. In addition, principals as provocateurs must ask themselves which teachers are really getting the job done and which ones have been hanging around simply because we lack the courage to address their weaknesses. All of this is dangerous territory for multiple reasons, but until our thoughts and beliefs are confronted, cycles of mediocrity will continue to plague our schools.

Lastly, the principal must be a statistician. As Sun Tzu said in the *Art of War*:

> "The general who wins a battle makes many calculations in his temple before the battle is fought. The general who loses a battle makes but few calculations beforehand. Thus do many calculations lead to victory, and few calculations to defeat: how much more if no calculation at all!"

In other words, the principal must understand data in order to make gains under our current accountability measures. Be it Adequate Yearly Progress or a waiver of NCLB, there are methods of calculating how students will perform on standardized tests well before the exam takes place. A few years ago, such methods were not as well-known, but principals in the 2000s and beyond should be able to predict with a great deal of certainty how their students will perform on the standardized tests months before the actual assessments are given. It is critical for the principal to learn how to calculate such information for himself so that the necessary planning can take place.

A New Day

A new day has arrived. At the end of that day, the principal is responsible for the academic achievement of students in that school. The principal can no longer be the chief disciplinarian of the school. His or her talents are now needed to oversee a living, functioning instructional process that must be attended to with a laser-sharp focus every day, all day.

There was a time when many principals spent their entire days in the office doing who knows what. We would often call it the "who knows what" paperwork. In addition, a lot of time would, and still is, spent dealing with disciplinary matters and providing support for faculty.

As I grew as a professional, I grew from being a traditional principal to a progressive one. I became an instructional leader. I developed a list of the top five things I did daily prior to and after becoming an instructional leader.

School Genetics: A Blueprint for Saving Public Schools

BEFORE becoming the Instructional Leader	AFTER becoming the Instructional Leader
1. Discipline 2. Meeting with Parents 3. Checking Email 4. Supervision/Duty 5. Signing Paperwork	1. Working with Professional Learning Communities (PLCs) 2. Observing Classrooms 3. Analyzing Data for Improvement 4. Supervision/Building Relationships 5. Reflecting on Practice

The AFTER column reflects a change in my thinking and actions after working with a former principal and very strong mentor. I changed my professional genetics so that I could be of service to the school's genetic makeup. If you notice, supervision is listed in both columns, but in two different ways. I used to be on post for duty, but I was not cultivating relationships. No matter how busy we are, principals must be visible to the stakeholders, especially those found inside of the building. This leads to building relationships that are healthy for students and teachers. Relationships matter. Students must know that you care about them. If they realize this, then they will comply. Teachers are your greatest commodity, and you must build bridges of trust and respect if you expect for them to work smarter and harder than in the past. When properly positioned, supported, and encouraged, teachers will go the extra distance if they believe in your cause. Do not confuse these statements with being liked by your stakeholders. As my mentor once told me, "If God was running for President, there would still be those who would vote for the devil." Building relationships is about building the needed respect and trust to get the right work done. Once those relationships are set, then the principal can begin developing and growing the team(s) necessary to lead to school improvement.

School Genetics: A Blueprint for Saving Public Schools

No Lone Rangers

The principal cannot go about saving schools alone. Once the principal is in a position, he or she must set about putting the right people in the right places. In rare cases, principals are able to create their schools from the ground up and hire everyone in the building. This is a truly remarkable opportunity because the principal is directly responsible for creating the professional culture and direction of the school. Hiring and knowing when to terminate faculty and staff is one of the most important jobs of the principal, and it is a reflection of the principal's ability to make sound decisions. The success (or failure) of that school rests solely upon the shoulders of the person who hired the people who work in that type of school.

In most cases, however, principals inherit the faculty and staff that have been there prior to his or her arrival. This can often be a challenge. The staff can take the mentality that, "Oh we will outlast him," and "I have seen principals come and go." While there is certainly some truth in many cases, the focus must remain not on who is at the helm of the school, but what the right work should be for children. Teachers who choose to remain stuck on the principal, and his or her style can cause resistance and hinder any movements toward the best instructional practice. Using the aforementioned traits above, the principal must find ways to get the support and effort of all faculty members. Also, the principal must find the members of the faculty who wish for school improvement. One common belief is that if a school is failing, the best thing to do is to remove all of the teachers and start over. Having served in two low performing settings and having seen turnarounds take place in both, I am a firm believer that there are members of any faculty who possess the skill sets and desire to improve their schools. The key is identifying the right ones and empowering them to do the right work.

My experience has been that when a person in the general society hears of schools that are considered failing, one natural response is a call to fire everyone in that building. I would contend that if the right leader looks closely, she will find many very talented persons in the building who not only care deeply about the school but also have the skill sets necessary to make positive changes. In my experiences in both of my previous principalships, I found persons who were extremely capable of leading school improvement and who were waiting for someone to guide their work.

School Genetics: A Blueprint for Savings Public Schools focuses heavily on school improvement, which is coordinated primarily at the leadership level. Student achievement, however, must take place at the teacher level. As has been stated earlier, the teacher is the number one factor in increasing student achievement. Every parent wants their children to be taught by good teachers. The best principal is no good if he or she does not have good teachers. In fact, if the teachers are perceived to be good, then the school is often perceived to be good. Thus, it behooves us to identify characteristics of good teachers.

LESSON 3

GOOD TEACHERS: ESSENTIAL BUILDING BLOCKS FOR GOOD SCHOOLS

Content Connections

What makes a good teacher? There are dozens of traits that a good teacher must possess, but there are two very important traits that I have observed that consistently lead to success. First, the teacher must be able to make content matter relevant and applicable to predictable and unpredictable situations so that the information can be used for student attainment and achievement. When I first wrote this statement, I simply said that a teacher must be able to teach content. In our digital age, content is already at the fingertips of anyone who chooses to access it from a host of search engines and websites. Knowledge itself is now a free commodity that can be obtained by anyone at any time. The distribution of knowledge is typically known as "teaching." Teaching is sharing information that a person does not know, and thereby, taking that person to a place of enhancing his or her knowledge base. Teaching used to be a process in which the "teacher" gives closely guarded, privately held content to the student (or "teachee"). Before the Internet, students had to get information from teachers who issue books to students for nearly a year and then collect those same books for the next year's class to haveaccess to the same knowledge. Now, this same information and rapidly expanding new information is available to all people anytime. Hence, although the teacher still functions in the role of teaching, it must be understood that academic teaching now takes place at an exponential rate independent of the teacher. Therefore, the shift for educators is not to focus on the "teacher *teaching*," but instead focus on "student *learning*." The important outcome of education is the learning, not the teaching. A savvy teacher must spend significantly more time getting students to understand *why* and *how* and less time focusing on the *what*. The "what" can be found through the teacher, books, and technology, but the "*why*" and "*how*" involve complex thought processes that challenge a person's current state of understanding, and which enhances the student's depth of knowledge and competency level. The older a student becomes, the more important it is for the teacher to be able to explain and develop "content connections." A person who is strong in content alone may not be adept at making students good learners. Therefore, they must know how to *engage* their students with the best instructional practices. Good teachers embrace technology and help students use it as a tool to acquire and understand the knowledge they are presented and how to best utilize that new knowledge. Good teachers not only show students how to think, create, and solve problems, but they also teach students how to forecast potential problems and create solutions for issues that do not even exist yet. Most of all, good teachers inspire students to actually care about the subject matter. The only way to do that is through the development of strong relationships between the teacher and the student.

School Genetics: A Blueprint for Saving Public Schools

All too often, an observer sees a teacher lecturing to his heart's content while the students sit quietly in the room, serving as nothing more than academic zombies waiting for the bell to ring. Again: the focus in classrooms must shift from powerful *teaching* to powerful *learning*. If a teacher teaches something to a student that he or she already knows, then teaching has not taken place. Teaching occurs only when a person learns something that he or she did not already know. Students only care to know about something if a connection can be made.

The statements found in this lesson about instruction are not original or new information. The first declaration that must be stated is that "best practice" in teaching and learning has existed for decades. Research documented and conducted since the late 1800s indicates how we learn and how we best process and master new information (Kliebard, 1995). Over the last century, research-based best practices have been presented in numerous ways that lead to better learning. This is important to acknowledge because in our efforts to find the "silver bullet" for learning, processes for teaching children effectively have already been discovered and used for years. Despite this, educators are constantly exposed to the sensation that their district and school level administrators are forcing "one more new thing" into their classrooms, when in truth educators are only being reminded of best practice that works. For example, John Dewey (Kliebard, 1995) taught us how important a hands-on experience is to creating and solving problems of a complex nature, and Madeline Cheek Hunter taught us how to create effective lesson plans in the 20th centu-

School Genetics: A Blueprint for Saving Public Schools

ry. While new methodologies continue to surface that help teachers do their jobs better, the research-based practices that lead to a high yield of student learning have already been recognized and should be found in most classrooms if the teacher is responsible and dedicated to the art and science of teaching (Marzano, et.al, 2001).

Yet, we constantly see that many teachers, despite knowing better and having been exposed to the best practices for teaching and learning, devolve into a lecture-based, desks-in-rows, worksheet driven classroom. The students passively sit and "listen," and fortunately, have not revolted and overpowered the poor teacher with their numbers. Why does this continue to happen? Why, even under the pressure of administrative warnings, political mandates, and expressed parental concerns does marginal teaching keep occurring in classroom after classroom? This is the true picture of teacher ineffectiveness. Teacher ineffectiveness is a virus that damages the genetic structure of a school. There are many, many reasons for this, but I will share the ones that I have personally observed to be rather prevalent:

1. Teacher Evaluation Models--As a nation, we are still struggling with the process of creating a truly useful and user-friendly teacher evaluation program. First, administrators currently vary in their skill sets, so what is good practice to one leader is poor practice to another, and this problem will not subside until all administrators become highly trained instructional leaders who share a common language in the area

of teaching and learning. Next, some evaluation systems are so broad in design that teachers must be absolutely deficient in their craft to get unsatisfactory marks. In other cases, the evaluation system is so cumbersome and convoluted that administrators drown in the paperwork while trying to complete the evaluation with fidelity. Thus, many evaluation systems fall victim to the Goldilocks "Porridge Effect;" the evaluation instrument is either too hot or too cold, but never just right. On top of that, teacher tenure and unions can make the process of dismissing, or even addressing marginal teachers for poor performance, an arduous task that is, quite honestly, avoided by many leaders. Lastly, administrators do not often monitor and observe classrooms to the degree necessary to accurately gauge the level of effectiveness of a teacher. Administrators perform numerous roles and answer to many stakeholders both internally and externally, and these tasks can pull even the best intentioned leader from the monitoring process. School and district leaders must find ways to remove barriers to make teacher observation a priority if there is any chance of improving instruction in classrooms.

2. Teacher Knowledge--Teacher lack of content knowledge is an elephant in the room that plagues schools across America. It is a sad fact that many teachers do not know their content to a degree in which they can convey accurate knowledge to children. This is highly evident in math classrooms. I have sat

through many professional learning experiences in which the adult learners sit quietly and pretend that they understand what is being taught, when in truth they are lost. Too many adult learners are afraid to be vulnerable and admit that they don't understand. This is not entirely the teacher's fault; some curricula are not teacher-friendly and do not lend themselves to efficient use. Once training is over, these same teachers go back to their classrooms, close the door, and resume providing the same mediocre instruction as they did the day before.

3. Teacher Time--There are only 24 hours in a day. Many teachers struggle with balancing the development of high quality, rigorous lessons, executing these lessons in the often less-than-one-hour per subject that is allotted, and coping with the myriad of other duties that a teacher must oversee. The situation becomes worse if there is poor classroom management. I remember talking with an elementary teacher who worked at a school that would be considered by most observers as dysfunctional. The students were unruly, and the school leadership did not provide much help. The teacher, who stated that she cried in the parking lot each morning before heading into the building, expressed that in one hour she may be able to get 10 to 15 minutes of decent instruction in her class. In these cases, teaching at a basic low level has become a survival technique for the teacher. The teacher is on the defensive, trying

to make it through another day and hoping that something will miraculously change on its own.

The infection known as teacher ineffectiveness has an antidote, however. Highly developed lesson planning, often vetted in strong professional learning communities, leads to better quality instruction. Teachers cannot underestimate the power of developing a detailed, intentionally thought-out lesson plan that reflects high yield research-based instructional practices. A well-crafted lesson plan serves as the road map for the execution of the next week's lessons. This is the best weapon for providing a high quality teaching and learning environment. A well-developed lesson focuses on students learning more so than teachers teaching. It is a blend of basic skills and higher-order, rigorous problem solving and innovation. A teacher who can develop and execute a solid lesson plan is well on the way to creating a learning environment that "cures" classrooms of marginal education and lackluster learning experiences.

In addition to teaching content, teachers must also teach appropriate behavior. I tell students all of the time, "Grades alone will not get you the ideal job or solely allow you to keep it. Your social skills are very important in making good lasting impressions and building professional relationships." Despite this well-known observation, we still find that many teachers have not been thoroughly taught and trained how to provide effective classroom management. Being able to control discipline so that learning is improved is the heart of being a master teacher. Classroom management is essential to enhancing the culture (school genetics) of a school. A strong teacher must know how to control the classroom. There are many models one can study, but I must state that Positive Behavioral Interventions and Supports (PBIS) has proven to be effective in the schools I have worked with--more will be shared about that process later in the book.

Reading

Early learning literacy is critical for students to achieve in school. Students must be exposed to a very rich world of speaking, reading, listening, and writing at an early age. Just as an athlete who is slower than his competitors must train twice as hard to compete; students who are behind in reading must be exposed at an even greater rate to catch them up to their peers. Students come to school with background knowledge based on their experiences (Marzano, 2004). We want children to be equipped with academic background knowledge. This type of knowledge fosters opportunity for students to learn and retain information at a higher rate. We have found that field trips and mentoring are excellent ways for children to increase their academic background knowledge, but these methods require both time and money that may be in short supply. When field trips and mentors are not enough, building a strong vocabulary is essential for building background knowledge. Vocabulary acquisition is critical for success. Students must be taught to not only recall words, but actually comprehend, evaluate, explain, defend, and/or justify what they read.

School Genetics: A Blueprint for Saving Public Schools

Students must be exposed to a variety of genres in reading, particularly informational, or nonfiction reading, so that they can be competitive globally. Educators should not underestimate the power of pictures, or nonlinguistic representations when teaching children to read. Images are powerful ways to communicate messages and bridge learning gaps for many children. Finally, we cannot forget the importance of writing. Writing is a skill that is often neglected when teachers and schools are crunched for time. Writing assignments take longer to grade, and some teachers choose to give fewer writing assignments for that reason. Writing is at the heart of a rigorous literacy program and cannot be compromised for time. We must find ways to keep writing alive in our curricula.

Social studies and science are wonderful courses in which literacy best practices must be infused. As a former science teacher, I have learned that if a child cannot comprehend, they are often unable to get the full benefit of scientific content. The same is true with social studies. Instead of teaching these subjects in isolation, I encourage all teachers to teach their content from a literacy perspective in an effort to improve a student's overall appreciation and confidence for reading.

Mathematics

In the area of math, I challenge educators to remember one key word with mathematics: BALANCE. Math is a subject that requires both basic skills and higher-order problem solving. A strong math program cannot exist without both

School Genetics: A Blueprint for Saving Public Schools

of these parts. In keeping with the theme, it is now appropriate to talk about how worksheets play a role in the concept of school genetics. When a person has an illness, drugs are often prescribed as a form of treatment. Worksheets are akin to a drug; they may relieve a problem, but can be abused too heavily, thus becoming an addiction. Worksheets, however, were created for a reason. In fact, they are still being created for a reason even though many would have you to believe that they are no longer fashionable (as a matter of fact, downright taboo). Worksheets, when used properly, have a role to play in instruction. Worksheets can be good for reinforcing skills. Worksheets were never intended to be the teacher. The key is not to use worksheets as a crutch and the entire instructional program. They should never be used as just "busy work." Even children in elementary grades can smell a "busy work" worksheet a mile away. By themselves, worksheets don't extend learning. Teachers must use their professional judgment to discern how to best use worksheets so that they enhance learning and make the students more proficient in the lesson being taught. Any other use is educational malpractice.

Another key observation about math teachers is that few of them are bonafide mathematicians. Herein lies the problem with math education in schools: math teachers are often not able to teach math deeply, even though they may know the methodology to help students learn. Mathematicians, on the other hand, have deep understanding of the content, but they may lack the ability to convey meaning to students, much less convey the passion for math that the mathematician may have. Often, math teachers are assumed to be able to teach all aspects of math (examples including algebra, geometry, statistics, calculus, etc.) when they may be proficient in only one or a few of these subjects. School leaders would be wise to recruit and select math teachers with great scrutiny and discretion. There is a shortage of high quality math teachers, and this fact should compel more school districts to find innovative ways to attract the best math teachers and retain them in their districts. Finally, mathematics is still a course that requires strong literacy skills. Math is all about reasoning. To reason well, a student must be an effective communicator in both written fashion and orally.

Other Subjects

In the age of college and career readiness, the importance of experential courses, physical education, fine arts, and foreign languages have never been more critical. A well-rounded student must have exposure to both core and extracurricular academic content. Literacy and numeracy skills can be taught and enhanced in extracurricular courses, and schools would be wise to promote electives, arts, and academics in these programs. Students have long since realized that people who make the most money in our society often are entertainers and athletes, so it would be irresponsible not to find value in these courses. In fact, these courses are critical to improving the Appearance portion of a school's genetic structure. Quality athletic programs and highly successful clubs are sources of inspiration for schools and the community. Great attention needs to be paid to these classes as they help improve the image of a school. More importantly, these courses educate the whole child. I once heard a superintendent present the need for elective courses along with academic courses in this manner, "You cannot have the core (academic subjects) without the Encore(extracurricular and electives)." In fact, these courses are critical to improving the Appearance portion of a school's genetic structure. Quality athletic programs and highly successful clubs are sources of inspiration for schools and the community. Attention needs to be paid to these classes as they help improve the image of a school.

Technology

Technology has already been referenced, but here are a few more thoughts. The world of education has changed forever and will be forever changing at an exponential rate. When I first became a teacher, I used a chalkboard. I graduated to a white board with dry erase markers, and my staff today now uses interactive projectors that open the entire world to their students. Within a few years, even this technology will become obsolete. We are in the midst of an epic societal disruption known as the Information Era, but we still have educators who are reluctant to embrace the inevitable new way of life for us all.

My advice about technology is to remember who the master is. We own technology, and we cannot allow the technology to own us. We must help our students understand the context behind the content that technology provides. Humans will still be needed for interpretation of content and mentoring students in the effective use of information.

Technology allows for us to do our work better. Technology involves tools often needed to discover and find answers to problems, but those discoveries must be guided by humans to help students find meaning and relevance in their work. Teachers must serve as the moral compass for children in a world that no longer has secrets. We must be technologically responsible and teach our children decent standards of being able to harness the power of technology with grace and civility. Our children are completely "plugged in," and admittedly, so are we as adults. Therefore, it is best for us to walk side-by-side, teacher and student, and explore this brave new world of access and possibility as a team. Again, teachers are people who "teach" others things they do not already know. As such, teachers must show students how to display appropriate etiquette and restraint when using technology and to focus their creative energies on solving world problems and making society better.

Passion: The Common Core of Relationships

If strong content knowledge and masterful delivery of content represent the "brain" of being a good teacher, the "heart" of a good teacher is passion. In a world in which students are socially connected to people 24 hours a day, the teacher has to find a way to make his or her voice relevant. Whereas, content knowledge and delivery can be taught and honed, passion is innate. Passion is what drives teachers to go above and beyond the call of duty. It is what compels teachers to intuitively know each of their students and know how to relate to them. Passion allows for strong, healthy relationships to be built, and students often respond to a teacher who shows care and patience. Passion drives teachers to give students a high-quality learning experience and not the mundane, routine stand-and-deliver lecture session every day. Passion drives a teacher to develop well-thought, research-based, carefully crafted lesson plans that serve as a roadmap for effective teaching and learning for the upcoming week. Passion is needed for teachers to develop a "whatever it takes" mentality that compels them to go above and beyond the call of duty and to implement programs with fidelity. Passion is what drives teachers to remain open-minded and optimistic about the profession and willing to work at improving their craft. Passion fuels good teachers to keep going when there is nothing left. Passion keeps teachers from making crippling excuses that impact their ability to maximize their effectiveness with students and colleagues.

High Expectations

School genetics is often best reflected in the culture of the school. Previously, I shared ideas about how the Appearance and Health of the school influenced how the community perceived the institution. The heart of this book is rooted in the conveyance of high expectations. High expectations must permeate throughout a school and the school district. This is more than just high expectations between a teacher and student. This is the interconnectedness among district leaders, board members, the community, administrators, teachers, parents, and students. Everyone must hold everyone else accountable. There is no one-sided coin of accountability. We all are responsible for the betterment of our schools. But what do high expectations really look like? This is a common definition problem. Sometimes we think we are displaying high expectations for someone, but actually we may be demonstrating something else. Here are a few thoughts to ponder.

First, high expectations involve setting realistic individualized goals for persons/ groups and providing the necessary support to help them reach that goal. They may reach that goal at different times in different ways, but the standard for meeting that expectation is held the same. Support in reaching the goal is absolutely necessary. Clarity in explaining the goal is absolutely necessary. Remembering NOT to lower the bar when the person struggles to achieve is absolutely necessary.

In the previous paragraph, I mentioned the word "realistic." The goal will never be realistic if there is not adequate ongoing support. Support comes in numerous ways. Schools need money in order to function and provide high quality services, and high quality usually involves having access to the appropriate support personnel. A school district needs the ability to be innovative without having to sell its soul in exchange for flexibility. Teachers need administrators who can offer them resources to get the job done and still hold them accountable for their work. Teachers also need parents who will allow for them to do their jobs professionally and students who value the benefits that come from hard work and effort. To hold high expectations among stakeholders means to be very intentional in thinking about what your expectations are. Do you know exactly what you want to see occur? What will it look like? How will you know when it has occurred? What have you provided by word and/or deed to ensure that you get to that goal? Holding high expectations for someone involves reflection, time, commitment, and sacrifice by all affected parties. It is not easy. It must be deliberate and incredibly focused. You must begin with the end in mind if you want someone to independently achieve a goal.

Having high expectations is very much individualized for each student in the classroom. All too often, a teacher must teach a classroom of children who have differing backgrounds, experiences, and beliefs about education. One public school core academic teacher supervises anywhere between eighteen to thirty-plus students at any one given point of time each day. Not many other professionals operate in such a manner. A physician typically sees one patient at a time and is able to focus on the needs of that one individual. An engineer will deal with one project at a time and create a plan of action for that one project. Law enforcement officers often work in teams when dealing with an alleged perpetrator or large groups of people. A waiter deals with each table individually, taking individual orders and providing service as needed for each patron. Teachers, however, have mostly been trained to teach all students at one time. The result has often led to a teaching "down the middle" approach that addresses most students' needs but leaves some lost and others bored. For any person to reach full potential, they will most likely benefit from direct, one-on-one instruction all day every day. This is not a promotion for home schooling or any other form of isolated education; the classroom is a social platform that educates children on how to collaborate, communicate, and learn the implicit and explicit societal rules to being a part of a community, and that should never be lost. People need people. But at the end of the day, if one is to fairly communicate high expectations to a person, time must be afforded to effectively communicate specific feedback to each individual person so that he or she is able to self-assess and grow from the experience.

In schools, we often miss opportunities or outright fail at conveying high expectations by our words and actions. That is because we rarely have professional development experiences reminding us of how our communication styles are intentionally and unintentionally transmitted to students. Both verbal and nonverbal communications send messages to children who then use that message to define their self-worth and ability. If I smile at a student, I may boost their self-confidence. If I cross my arms or roll my eyes, I may display disgust to a child, even if I was thinking about something else entirely. We must be mindful that our behavior, language, dress code, and attitude influence students' behavior. I have found that many adults in today's pop culture often speak and dress like students, and by doing so, we have unintentionally lowered our expectations to meet their lifestyle. We must give them something to aspire to become, which means holding ourselves at a standard for them to rise to our level. The master teacher knows how to bridge that generational gap by relating to today's student but still setting the standard for responsible, professional adult conduct.

School Genetics: A Blueprint for Saving Public Schools

As a related side note, I would like to tell you a story about our family dog, Morocco. Morocco is a Yorkshire Terrier, a small toy dog. One wintery night, I let Morocco go outside in the backyard. He saw four deer in the yard and began barking and chasing them. All four deer ran away with Morocco in pursuit. As I called for him to come back, it hit me: Morocco chased them off bravely because no one ever told him how small he was. In Morocco's eyes, he is a fierce warrior and giant protector of his home. Research has shown that students who do not know their limitations are capable of stretching their mindset to do great things (Dweck, 2006). In addition, we sometimes have to "speak life" into students by encouraging and motivating them to do what would have otherwise been unachievable by them. This is not to be confused with over-the-top unnecessary praise. Students need to understand realistic goals and get "tough love" at times so that they know what struggle feels like. They need to learn how to self-assess their progress so that they can set new attainable goals for their next steps. Again, the master teacher knows how to balance both constructive praise and realistic expectations for the benefit of his or her students.

In short, a good teacher must possess a brain for content skill and delivery and a heart made of passion for the profession. I will not purport how much "brain" or how much " heart" is needed to make a good teacher--I would simply say that both are needed in great demand. If an educator is lacking one of these two key ingredients, the result is an ineffective teacher every time.

LESSON 4

PROFESSIONAL LEARNING COMMUNITIES

A good teacher alone is a remarkable thing, but the best teaching and learning comes when groups of teachers work together to form Professional Learning Communities (PLCs). PLCs are essential to school improvement because they give educators the opportunity to share, discuss, and refine best instructional practices to meet the needs of all students. Historically, education has been a field of isolation; the one room schoolhouse had one teacher who created his or her own curriculum and taught what was needed for the time. Now, we are able to collaborate in manners that bring forth the best teaching experiences for children. This level of camaraderie fosters the "whatever it takes" mentality expressed by DuFour and others (DuFour et. al, 2004).

One of the most important goals of a Professional Learning Community is to establish common language among the educators in the district. For instance, if you ask ten educators to write the definition of RtI, you will probably get ten different answers. Much of the jargon we use has taken different contexts among the users, and district leaders must ensure that the beliefs, strategic plans, products, and processes used are familiar to employees in the schools. Any company that has found sustained success uses agreed-upon common language and has standard operating procedures that govern their actions. The same must be true in education. Professional learning communities provide teachers the time and opportunity to clarify terms, to mutually support how the terms are used, and to understand what those terms mean to that organization.

Whether teachers work in elementary, middle or high school levels, the master schedule must reflect common planning time. The master schedule is the secret weapon for school improvement because this is where we find time to do the tasks that need to be done for increased student achievement. As much as possible, teachers who teach the same subject and/or in the grade level must have time *during the school day* to meet and discuss best practices. "During the school day" is crucial. Effective professional learning is sometimes difficult to obtain before or after school hours because of teacher fatigue, after school responsibilities, and the personal lives of educators.

On the next page is a picture of a sample master schedule that features built-in common planning time for Newton High school social studies teachers when I served there.

School Genetics: A Blueprint for Saving Public Schools

Teacher	1st	2nd	3rd	4th	5th	6th	7th
A	American Gov Co (Special Ed CoTeacher)	American Gov	Instructional Focus	American Gov	American Gov	American Gov	
	45.8570000	45.0570000		45.0570000	45.0570000	45.0570000	COMMON PLANNING
B	Quest/ Adv American Gov	Quest/ Adv American Gov	Instructional Focus	Quest/ Adv American Gov	Quest/ Adv American Gov ALA 1	Quest/ Adv American Gov ALA 2	
	45.2570000	45.2570000		45.2570000	45.2570000	45.2570000	COMMON PLANNING
C	AP World History	AP World History	Instructional Focus	World History	AP World History	AP World History	
	45.0811000	45.0811000		45.0830000	45.0811000	45.0811000	COMMON PLANNING
D	American Gov	Current Issues	Instructional Focus	Psychology	World History	Sociology	
	45.0570000	45.0120000		45.0150000	45.0830000	45.0310000	COMMON PLANNING
E	World History	World History	Instructional Focus	World History	US History	US History	
	45.0830000	45.0830000		45.0830000	45.0810000	45.0810000	COMMON PLANNING
F	AP US History	AP US History	Instructional Focus	AP US History	US History	US History	
	45.0820000	45.0820000		45.0820000	45.0810000	45.0810000	COMMON PLANNING
G	US History	US History	Instructional Focus	US History	American Gov	US History	
	45.0810000	45.0810000		45.0810000	45.0570000	45.0810000	COMMON PLANNING
H	PLAN (Dept. Chair)	American Gov Co (Special Ed CoTeacher)	Instructional Focus	American Gov Co (Bledsoe)	American Gov Co (Special Ed CoTeacher)	American Gov Co	
		45.8570000		45.8570000	45.8570000	45.8570000	COMMON PLANNING
I	Econ Co (Special Ed CoTeacher)	Econ co (Special Ed CoTeacher)	Instructional Focus	AP ECONOMICS	Econ Co (Special Ed CoTeacher)	AP ECONOMICS	
	45.0610000	45.0610000		45.0620000	45.0610000	45.0620000	COMMON PLANNING
J	Econ	Econ	Instructional Focus	Econ	Econ	Econ	
	45.0610000	45.0610000		45.0610000	45.0610000	45.0610000	COMMON PLANNING
K	AP Psychology	American Gov	Instructional Focus	AP Psychology	World History	American Gov	
	45.0160000	45.0570000		45.0160000	45.0830000	45.0570000	COMMON PLANNING
L	US History Co- (Special Ed CoTeacher)	AP Government	Instructional Focus	US History Co (Special Ed CoTeacher)	US History Co (Special Ed CoTeacher)	US History Co (Special Ed CoTeacher)	
	45.0810000	45.0520000		45.0810000	45.0810000	45.0810000	COMMON PLANNING

School Genetics: A Blueprint for Saving Public Schools

The master schedule is integral in creating an environment in which students can learn at their maximum potential. Middle schools in Georgia promote common planning time, and many elementary schools have created similar schedules. High schools are usually the last great frontier in public education that implement change, so the example described here shows how it can be done in high school settings. At Newton High, our school operated on a seven-period schedule. All classes were 52-minutes in length. Six periods were credit-bearing courses, and the seventh period was called Instructional Focus period. This was a non-credit bearing period for most students except for those who wished to earn additional credits during the school year. For most students, this was a time for remediation or enrichment. The Instructional Focus period can be held at different times of the day, but we opted for third period, which was right before lunch. If Instructional Focus was first period, we realized that some students who drove might come to school late. Also, we were afraid some might try to leave campus early if we had Instructional Focus as the last period of the day (again, this is high school). It is easy for Instructional Focus to turn into a loosely designed study hall if not closely monitored and enforced, so the Leadership Team frequently observed instruction during this time to make sure Instructional Focus worked. This takes dedication and effort. After several iterations of the process, we created a schedule in which students rotated to their regular classes weekly each day during this time period. By doing this, students were typically given an additional class period to work on classroom studies with their teacher each week. This also allowed for teachers to earn an extra planning period each week, which was huge for teacher buy-in.

In addition to creating a master schedule that gives more time for children to get remediation and/or enrichment, the master schedule can allow for common planning time so that teachers form functioning Professional Learning Communities. Research and experience both support the notion that PLCs must not only have defined dates, times, and locations for meeting, but they should follow a prescribed agenda asking the following questions:

1. What do we want students to know, understand and be able to do? (Curriculum)
2. How do we best engage students in using research-based instructional strategies and build their background knowledge? (Instruction)
3. How do we know that students have learned the concepts we teach? (Assessment)
4. What do we do if they do not meet these standards or if the work is not rigorous enough for them? (Response to Intervention)

I learned that teachers must remain focused on these topics and create lesson plans that reflect these questions, if strategic teaching and learning is to take place. A sample of guiding questions for a PLC agenda is shown on the next page.

School Genetics: A Blueprint for Saving Public Schools

Sample Professional Learning Community Meeting Questions

Professional Learning Community Guiding Questions

1. Data

    a. What data have we collected since the last meeting?
    b. Are there any patterns that we can see in the data?
    c. How can this data help drive the instructional process?
    d. What strategies can we develop to remediate or enrich based on this data?

2. Collaborative Planning

    a. What do we want students to know, do, and understand (Curriculum/ Standards)?
    b. How do we best engage students in the learning (Research Based Instructional Strategies)?
    c. How do we know if students know, do and understand what we want (Assessments- Formative and Summative)?
    d. What do we do if students don't know, do, and understand what we want (Remediation and enrichment)?

School Genetics: A Blueprint for Saving Public Schools

One of the best strategies for a PLC to conduct is to observe a teacher(s), PLC, or school that is doing something well. This is an activity that is of relatively low cost. Model teachers should be identified in the school that can teach others how to perform a particular strategy or process. If that teacher cannot be found in the school, traveling to other schools may be needed for teachers to learn how to perform a strategy. The best way to teach an adult learner is for him or her to see what is expected firsthand. The best classes/schools to observe are those with similar demographics as your school--it helps to see others in your situation accomplish goals with the same set of barriers. This also reduces excuses and changes paradigms for skeptics. Principals and school leaders must take efforts to expose staff to the best practitioners available so that expectations are clear and excuses are removed.

LESSON 5

LEADERSHIP IS A TEAM SPORT

If schools have genetics, and if one wishes to improve genetic structure, leadership teams are a necessary treatment. One of the most important steps in fixing schools is the establishment of leadership teams. Leadership teams go by a wide variety of names, and please understand that there will most likely be several types of leadership teams within the school. For example, schools I served had the following teams:

1. Administrative Team-consisting of me the principal and assistant principals
2. Design Team-an instructional team whose focus was on the instructional plan of the school
3. Response to Intervention Team (RtI)-focused on ensuring students who needed extra support received that support
4. Discipline Team-dedicated to school culture and climate

Each of these teams functioned as "executive level" professional learning communities. We had set agendas with set dates, times, and locations for meetings. This is important so that we were not distracted from the work that needed to take place. Norms for meeting must also be established. This is not a time for whining or complaining, but is a time for problem solving and solution finding.

Sample of Meeting Norms

1. Attend and participate in all meetings.
2. All discussions are to be treated as confidential unless given express permission from the principal or his/her designee.
3. Respect all opinions and be open to new ideas.
4. Refrain from side conversations and distracting behaviors.
5. Leave each meeting with new information and/or actions to implement.

Administrative Team

Every administrative team is different. Some schools only have the principal and one assistant principal. Some schools have several assistant principals. Regardless of the configuration, this team is necessary for setting the direction, practices, and policies of the school. The instructional work does not get done here, but its importance should not be underestimated. The best piece of advice I could give school leaders about the administrative team is that they must be unified. As the old saying goes, "If the head is weak, then the body will soon follow." There must be a united front among administrators if there is any chance for school improvement to occur and be sustained. It is important for the school culture that they see the administrative staff on one accord. This team needs to meet weekly so that all school leaders are clear about what is happening in the building. The more the administrative team is seen together publicly, the stronger the team becomes. It is too difficult to "divide and conquer" when the administrative team is together. In the most ideal situation, the principal will clearly be recognized as the instructional leader of the school. Discipline should be primarily handled by assistant principals with the principal being available to hear appeals from parents when necessary. If the principal is not the instructional leader, an assistant principal of instruction is needed to work in close tandem with the principal to ensure that the right work is carried out on the principal's behalf. At the end of the day, the principal is responsible for the achievement of her students, so it is critical that these relationships are strong and in constant harmony.

The Hand: NHS Administrative Team, 2011-2013

School Genetics: A Blueprint for Saving Public Schools

A key component for furthering success of an administrative team is a very well defined organizational chart of primary duties that is divided among administrators. Administrators must "know their role" in the school, and staff must be clear who to contact when issues occur. Here is an organizational chart used at Newton High:

Sample Administrative Organizational Chart

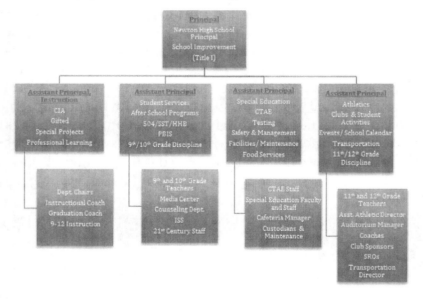

Design Team

In the business of school improvement, the most important team beyond the administrative team is the instructional team. A common name for such teams is "Design Team," or the team that is responsible for the instructional design of the school. Selection of members for this team is of the utmost importance. **_The principal must identify people who have demonstrated that they can focus only on the things that lead to increased student achievement and more effective teaching._** The Design Team must be filled with critical thinkers who can identify problems and diagnose numerous ways to find solutions that are practical and effective in addressing the issue. The only way to grow from basic thinking is for healthy discourse to take place among the Design Team members. This means that the Design Team should be prepared to meet weekly and dedicate sufficient time to properly vet matters of importance. This sort of conversation often leads to the professional growth of all members, and a collective groupthink about what really matters becomes prevalent. The team becomes more important than the individual, and the school benefits from the synergy thus created among team members.

WARNING: It is critical to point out that the Design Team (and all leadership teams, for that matter) is not to be a team merely for team's sake. This group cannot simply rubber stamp the principal's decisions. A group of "yes men" will not advance the school. This is a team that weighs options and lands on the most viable solution. A leader must be able to spark conversation and seek consensus on issues. An experienced principal who has led school transformation may be able to suggest a few courses of action, but the best process is when the team creates their action steps through collaboration <u>based on evidence</u>. Evidence must drive the team's decisions, never emotion. This means that egos must be checked at the door. Again, a skillful leader can guide teams to an acceptable choice, but the team must own the problem if positive legitimate action is to occur. The leader must be receptive and open to criticism and let the team support the work. This requires the leader to be able to "let go" and turn over some authoritative decision-making to the team.

The Design Team is the group that collects and analyzes data to determine the need for changes. This group oversees the Data Room, a room that showcases formative and summative data that is used to design strategies and interventions for classroom use.

Why a data room? The data room keeps the relevant issues right in front of you. There are a host of issues that arise in schools, and any one of them can distract school leaders from focusing on student achievement. The data room should remain in a constant state of flux, and new data that is created must be used to inform schools of practices needed to help students and teachers. The data room is command central, the headquarters, the war room, and the situation room. A "living" data room serves to educate and inform the Design Team on how to tackle issues that the team addresses.

Land Mine: The creation of a data room often sputters, even though many schools see its value. Why? Time must be dedicated to its creation. It usually takes <u>one eight-hour work day</u> provided that "starter" data is readily available. Starter data includes the most recent standardized test information; attendance data; discipline data; school and/or district strategic plans; and any other data that will help the school maintain its focus on student achievement. Examples of data that could be posted in the data room can be found below.

Data Room Artifacts

Just like decorating a room in your home, the data room must be created with a sense of purpose that displays the character and direction of the school. From that point, it must evolve regularly to meet the challenges that the school faces.

Action Plans- Work on the Focus, then Focus on the Work

The single most important task of the Design Team is to ensure that actions are focused and addressed in a timely manner. To this end, the Design Team created action plans that helped us remain on target.

School Genetics: A Blueprint for Saving Public Schools

Tips for creating effective actions plans:

1. Never select more than five action items to accomplish within a nine-week period.
2. Some action items are large-scale goals. Such goals may carry on from one period to the next. With these action items, the goal is to reach a sense of completion by the end of the school year or be prepared to address the items again the next school year.
3. Add action items that are "quick wins" for the school to accomplish. Quick wins keep the team motivated because they can see tangible results. As the old saying goes, "success builds success."
4. Color-coding items to show what has been accomplished, what is in progress, and what has not been done helps keep the team focused. See the plan as an example.
5. Every meeting must revolve around the action plan. If it does not, then the plan should have never been created. Stay focused on the action plan and its execution.

A sample Action Plan can be found on the next page.

School Genetics: A Blueprint for Saving Public Schools

Actions, Strategies, and Interventions	Timeline	Person(s) Responsible	Means of Evaluation	
			Artifacts/Materials	Additional Comments/ Next Steps
	January 2013	Teachers, Principal, AP1, Academic Coaches, Dept. Chairs	Essential Questions Standards, Word Walls, SB Bulletin Boards, centers, student work, exemplars, Quad training	
	3rd 9 weeks	Design Team, ELA Dept., Teachers, Academic Coaches	25 Books Campaign posters, eReaders, books, essay grading technology	

In summary, the principal benefits from a highly engaged, active instructional design team that represents a cross section of educators who are invested in the improvement of the school. They must meet at least once a week to develop the synergy and skills necessary to make the school better. Weekly meetings are non-negotiable. The team must focus on data and create action plans that keep it focused on the right work. The actions described in this single section will lead to an improved school more than any other single action that the principal could perform.

The next team that we need to focus on is the Response to Intervention (RtI) Team. The administrative team oversees the entire school and the Design Team focuses on the instructional program, but the RtI team drills down to the individual student needs.

RtI has different meanings to different educators. For me, RtI is an intentional response to student differences (i.e., interventions) that have been determined by formative and summative assessments. Pretend that a student is a patient going to a physician's office. The patient (student) has a cough, and the physician (teacher) must diagnose the cause of the cough and then provide the appropriate treatment. Once diagnosed, the treatment is used until it is determined if it works. If the treatment is working, then the physician either ends the treatment or continues the treatment as needed. If the treatment is not working, then new tests should be conducted, and a new treatment, possibly more aggressive, is used to remedy the cough.

In schools, the same practice is effective in helping students. Surprisingly, though, this does not happen as often as needed. Why? The answer is pretty simple: while a physician is usually treating one patient at a time, teachers have at least twenty students in their presence at any one given time, so individualized attention becomes difficult. Add to the 1:20 teacher:student ratio, other duties, paperwork, meetings, personal issues, and work-related burdens, it is an absolute marvel that a teacher can do much more than teach to the middle of the classroom. Teaching to the middle, however, only works for those in that bracket, and those who are higher achievers or in need of extra support are often left to their own devices. A structured school-wide RtI process can address the needs of individual students and thus move the school forward. The next two lessons show how to achieve those goals.

LESSON 6

TAYLOR COUNTY UPPER ELEMENTARY: THE JOURNEY FROM WORST TO FIRST

As the principal of Taylor County Upper Elementary School (TCUES), I served approximately 600 students in grades three through six. Often times, many students are identified as needing special education services very early in their school career, and many teachers have difficulty distinguishing between a child who is in need of special services or who has other factors that inhibit their ability to act and perform appropriately in classrooms. In TCUES, one out of every seven students was in special education programs during my tenure. During this time, the state standardized test that all students had to take in order to show proficiency levels that met or exceeded standards was the Criterion-Referenced Competency Test, or the CRCT. The national Adequate Yearly Progress interpretation in Georgia was that if one subgroup of students did not meet a certain benchmark, the entire school failed. The Students with Disabilities (commonly called SWDs) at TCUES had difficulty meeting this requirement, and the school became an NI-6 elementary school in the state of Georgia during my tenure. These were children the AYP reports were talking about, not numbers. The community did not deserve this, and I was determined to find a way to make this right.

School Genetics: A Blueprint for Saving Public Schools

This lesson will focus heavily on Response to Interventions, also known as RtI. RtI was the defining collection of practices that transformed Taylor County Upper Elementary and Newton High School to higher performing schools. RtI was the heart of school improvement in both of these settings. Response to Interventions is the closest thing to a "silver bullet" that I have practiced in which academic gains were evidenced. For the schools featured in this book, it was the heart of the school improvement process. Yet, I am amazed to see that many schools grapple with effective implementation of the RtI program. In efforts to demystify RtI and make it practical, the following sections describe what Response to Intervention practices were put into place to address the needs of the students and to improve their achievement.

In Georgia, the Response to Intervention pyramid is divided into four tiers, while many educators nationally recognize this pyramid as a three-tiered structure. Regardless of the design, the premise is basically the same. A team of educators must be assembled to adequately assess the programs and processes the school designates at each tiered level. I recommend the principal serve on the team. Other team members will be featured later. The RtI team must first identify what type of intervention a student may need. Schools can use universal screeners as a first step in determining student strengths and weaknesses. A universal screener in reading and math is typically a very quick user-friendly test that assesses the skills of students. Universal screeners can tell you if student deficiencies are individualized per student, or if they are classroom deficiencies in which the majority of the class needs help with particular concepts. It is very important to distinguish between classroom deficiencies and individual student deficiencies. If one child shows a skill deficit, then support can be offered to that one child in the appropriate area. If we see most or all of the class has the same deficiencies, however, it indicates an instructional problem. Often, class-wide deficiencies indicate a school or even a district wide deficiency, and this means that a curricular problem may have occurred at some point. At any rate, a screener gives teachers direction as to how to best help their students. The universal screeners are crucial in determining which students have greater needs and how to best support those students.

The next step for the school was to determine which interventions or strategies would support the different needs of the learners in the school. Schools often purchase numerous materials, and these materials are often shelved once the nuance wears off. We reviewed products in our school and began to classify the products in a "Pyramid of Interventions" model. The purpose of doing this was twofold: 1) so that we could ensure that we knew what actually was available to our teachers, and 2) so that we could establish a common language of practice for supporting students. When we hear the term "best practices," we often do not clarify what the best practices are, or what materials have been proven successful in helping students. By creating this visual chart, our staff knew what was commonly agreed upon as resources we used to support our students.

The first tier of the RtI pyramid is Tier 1, or the standards based classroom tier. This is the area in which 80% of all students should belong. This means that 80% of the students should respond positively to high-quality, strong classroom practices. This is good teaching. Virtually every student in the building should have access to these practices. Tier 1 should include a healthy variation of basic skills practice along with higher-order, or more rigorous, instruction. A common problem in classrooms is that many teachers, when not monitored, may attempt to include rigorous teaching in their classrooms, but eventually digress to teaching basic skills in a very traditional way. There are many reasons this occurs, both valid and not. I have found that many teachers struggle with the idea of what rigor is due to a lack of common understanding of the educational jargon we use. I am defining rigor as the use of higher-order skills commonly found in the higher level of Bloom's Taxonomy or levels two, three, or four of the Depth of Knowledge. While basic skills instruction focuses on memorization and recall, rigorous teaching focuses on the application, creation, and explanation. Teachers must remember that basic skills' teaching emphasizes the "What?," "When?," and "Where?," whereas rigorous, higher-order teaching emphasizes the "How?" and "Why?" Again, both basic skills training and rigorous teaching are needed. A skillful teacher must master these elements and interweave them as she takes students to a higher level of skill and academic independence. A weekly lesson plan should show where action verbs are clearly used that allow for students to perform a variety of tasks. In addition to high- quality teaching, there should be frequent assessment of student learning to show that students have mastered the concepts being taught.

These assessments should occur at least weekly in several formats so that the teacher knows that students are indeed grasping the material.

Academic Coaches

The RtI team at TCUES had two academic coaches who supervised the Tier 1 efforts at the school. These academic coaches did not have classroom responsibilities, so they were able to help teachers manage their workloads and get the right work done. The academic coach is a relatively new concept in educational staffing in many states. They go by a variety of names (e.g., instructional coach), but their primary role is to manage the instructional program in a school as the principal's designee. I have found that many principals do not see the value of academic coaches. Academic coaches, when used properly, are extremely beneficial to a school program. Great care needs to be taken in selecting an academic coach because that person heavily influences the instructional atmosphere of the school. The principal should serve as the instructional leader, but the academic coach carries out detailed work relative to instruction. Academic coach positions are often financed through federal programs, but I would encourage state legislation to add this position to its educational funding formula. I liken the academic coach position to the invention of the cell phone; once you have one, you cannot imagine life without it. These are neither clerical nor administrative roles; the focus must remain on improving instructional programs, modeling for teachers, providing professional learning, and offering classroom support for teachers.

School Genetics: A Blueprint for Saving Public Schools

Great academic coaches who are highly knowledgeable about teaching practices and who are able to build trust among teachers will move a school forward.

Tracking Student Progress and Formative Assessment

At TCUES, the RtI team created documents to help teachers track student progress. Best practice and solid research has proven that we must assess student academic growth very often to monitor if they are seeing academic success. This formative assessment must be tracked and intentionally studied if we are going to make instructional changes in the best interest of the child. Intentionality is crucial. It is too easy to test children ad nauseum only to file the results in a cabinet never to be seen again. We realized that we needed a manageable, teacher friendly way to keep ourselves accountable and aware of student progress. At TCUES, we did not have forms that helped us keep up with data, so we created them. One was the TCUES Instructional Plan. The basic idea was that every child had an instructional plan much like special education students have an Individualized Education Plan (IEP). While not as robust as an IEP, the Instructional Plan allowed for teachers, students, and parents to know how a child was progressing. A sample follows on the next page.

School Genetics: A Blueprint for Saving Public Schools

TCUES Student Instructional Plan
2008-2009

Name_____

Grade_____

The purpose of the student instructional plan is to inform students, parents, teachers and administrators of student progress on an ongoing basis.

Fall	Winter	Spring
____CRCT Math '07 ____CRCT Reading '07 ____DRA ____STAR Reading ____STAR Math Student Initials:_____ Teacher Initials:_____ Administrator Initials:_____	____# of books read ____DRA ____STAR Reading ____STAR Math Student Initials:_____ Teacher Initials:_____ Administrator Initials:_____	____# of books read ____CRCT Math '08 ____CRCT Reading '08 ____DRA ____Science Fair (6th gra) ____STAR Reading ____STAR Math Student Initials:_____ Teacher Initials:_____ Administrator Initials:_____

Passing Scores:

25 Books Campaign: Each child should read 1,000,000 words, or 25 books a year. Since book vary in length and complexity, the following model has been developed:
    3rd grade- 8 chapter books or 45 short books every nine weeks
    4th grade- 6 chapter books or 60 short books every nine weeks
    5th grade- 6 chapter books or 60 short books every nine weeks
    6th grade- 6 chapter books or 60 short books every nine weeks

CRCT math-   800

CRCT reading- 800

DRA Grade Level Scores
    3rd grade- 30
    4th grade- 40
    5th grade- 50
    6th grade- 60

Another document used at TCUES was the class target template. A sample of this document can be found on the next page. The template was used to classify students based upon their most recent standardized test score reports. This document was used to identify "bubble students," or students who were within ten points of failing an assessment or moving into the Exceeds category. While this was "dead data" that could not be changed, it was helpful in setting the stage as new formative assessments were being used. This information was kept in the data room but was placed in folders because there was personally identifiable information. The RtI team studied this information regularly so that we could know exactly how many students were in jeopardy and how we could specifically target the needs of those students. Other documents utilized at the Tier 1 level included reading and math profile sheets. These sheets were important because they not only informed the school of what level a student was performing, but also what, if any, supports were put in place to help them.

School Genetics: A Blueprint for Saving Public Schools

Class Target Template

CRCT Class Target Template Reading/ELA/Math 2008-2009				
School: <u>Taylor County Upper Elementary</u> **Grade:** _____				
Homeroom Teacher **# of students**				
Subject	700-774	775-799	800-824	824-849	+850
Reading					
ELA					
Math					

School Genetics: A Blueprint for Saving Public Schools

Another important feature of the Tier 1 program at Taylor County Upper Elementary was the emphasis on literacy. In Georgia, there was once a standard in which students had to read 25 books, or one million words, per year. We promoted this practice with the 25 Books Campaign program, in which we challenged students to meet certain reading goals by the end of the year. When the school met its reading goal, I had to perform a stunt at the end of the year, and this unified the school by creating a culture of reading. A sample chart for tracking their reading progress can be found on the next page.

School Genetics: A Blueprint for Saving Public Schools

25 Books Campaign Sheet

NAME:_____

3rd Grade Level K-P	4th Grade Level O-T	5th Grade Level S-W	6th Grade Level V-Y
1st Nine Weeks Reading goals: 8 Chapter OR 45 Short books Student Read: ____Chapter OR ____Short books Check one: ____Has Not Met ____Meets ____Exceeds	**1st Nine Weeks** Reading goals: 6 Chapter OR 60 Short books Student Read: ____Chapter OR ____Short books Check one: ____Has Not Met ____Meets ____Exceeds	**1st Nine Weeks** Reading goals: 6 Chapter OR 60 Short books Student Read: ____Chapter OR ____Short books Check one: ____Has Not Met ____Meets ____Exceeds	**1st Nine Weeks** Reading goals: 6 Chapter OR 60 Short books Student Read: ____Chapter OR ____Short books Check one: ____Has Not Met ____Meets ____Exceeds
2nd Nine Weeks Reading goals: 8 Chapter OR 45 Short books Student Read: ____Chapter OR ____Short books Check one: ____Has Not Met ____Meets ____Exceeds	**2nd Nine Weeks** Reading goals: 6 Chapter OR 60 Short books Student Read: ____Chapter OR ____Short books Check one: ____Has Not Met ____Meets ____Exceeds	**2nd Nine Weeks** Reading goals: 6 Chapter OR 60 Short books Student Read: ____Chapter OR ____Short books Check one: ____Has Not Met ____Meets ____Exceeds	**2nd Nine Weeks** Reading goals: 6 Chapter OR 60 Short books Student Read: ____Chapter OR ____Short books Check one: ____Has Not Met ____Meets ____Exceeds
3rd Nine Weeks Reading goals: 8 Chapter OR 45 Short books Student Read: ____Chapter OR ____Short books Check one: ____Has Not Met ____Meets ____Exceeds	**3rd Nine Weeks** Reading goals: 6 Chapter OR 60 Short books Student Read: ____Chapter OR ____Short books Check one: ____Has Not Met ____Meets ____Exceeds	**3rd Nine Weeks** Reading goals: 6 Chapter OR 60 Short books Student Read: ____Chapter OR ____Short books Check one: ____Has Not Met ____Meets ____Exceeds	**3rd Nine Weeks** Reading goals: 6 Chapter OR 60 Short books Student Read: ____Chapter OR ____Short books Check one: ____Has Not Met ____Meets ____Exceeds
4th Nine Weeks Reading goals: 8 Chapter OR 45 Short books Student Read: ____Chapter OR ____Short books Check one: ____Has Not Met ____Meets ____Exceeds	**4th Nine Weeks** Reading goals: 6 Chapter OR 60 Short books Student Read: ____Chapter OR ____Short books Check one: ____Has Not Met ____Meets ____Exceeds	**4th Nine Weeks** Reading goals: 6 Chapter OR 60 Short books Student Read: ____Chapter OR ____Short books Check one: ____Has Not Met ____Meets ____Exceeds	**4th Nine Weeks** Reading goals: 6 Chapter OR 60 Short books Student Read: ____Chapter OR ____Short books Check one: ____Has Not Met ____Meets ____Exceeds

School Genetics: A Blueprint for Saving Public Schools

Math was an area of particular trouble for us, so we created a form that allowed us to track student performance in math based upon the textbook we were using at the time. After analyzing so much data, we found that it was very easy to view a student as a number and not as a person. To help with this, we began placing yearbook photos on these forms so that we could remember that we were not treating scores, but children. Sample progress monitoring charts for math are found on the next two pages. These children come to us the best they know how, and we must always remember to treat them with dignity and respect. Again, these documents were kept in a secure place for our analysis.

School Genetics: A Blueprint for Saving Public Schools

```
Current Grade Level: 6
2007 CRCT Math: _____

[photo]

Math Teacher: _____
SWD (Y/N) _____  Exceptionality _____
Domain Weaknesses:


Pyramid of Intervention Tier: _____ Afterschool Tutoring: _____
Connections Teachers: _____ / _____ / _____ / _____
Mock CRCT Scores (October)_____ (December)_____ (February)_____
Math End-of-Unit Scores
    Prime Time_____   Bits & Pieces 1_____   Filling & Wrapping_____
    Bits & Pieces 2_____   Bits & Pieces 3_____   How Likely Is it?_____
    Data About Us_____   GPS Additonal Times_____
Comments:_____
_____
_____
_____
```

We tracked student math performance with the illustrated benchmark sheet. Every student had to have the equivalent of an individual learning plan so that we could monitor student progress.

School Genetics: A Blueprint for Saving Public Schools

Math Benchmarks Sheet

NAME:_____

Safety Net recommended any time the score is below 70%.
Safety Net Recommendations
    A. Small Group/Individual Instruction in Class
    B. Study Skills Class during Connections
    C. Student Support Services (SST)
    D. 21st Century After-school Program
    E. Supplemental Education Services (SES)
    F. Other (please specify):_____

3rd Grade	4th Grade	5th Grade	6th Grade
1st 9 Wks ____%	1st 9 Wks ____%	1st 9 Wks ____%	1st 9 Wks ____%
Safety Net? Y N If "Yes," then what safety net(s):_____	Safety Net? Y N If "Yes," then what safety net(s):_____	Safety Net? Y N If "Yes," then what safety net(s):_____	Safety Net? Y N If "Yes," then what safety net(s):_____
2nd 9 Wks ____%	2nd 9 Wks ____%	2nd 9 Wks ____%	2nd 9 Wks ____%
Safety Net? Y N If "Yes," then what safety net(s):_____	Safety Net? Y N If "Yes," then what safety net(s):_____	Safety Net? Y N If "Yes," then what safety net(s):_____	Safety Net? Y N If "Yes," then what safety net(s):_____
3rd 9 Wks ____%	3rd 9 Wks ____%	3rd 9 Wks ____%	3rd 9 Wks ____%
Safety Net? Y N If "Yes," then what safety net(s):_____	Safety Net? Y N If "Yes," then what safety net(s):_____	Safety Net? Y N If "Yes," then what safety net(s):_____	Safety Net? Y N If "Yes," then what safety net(s):_____
4th 9 Wks ____%	4th 9 Wks ____%	4th 9 Wks ____%	4th 9 Wks ____%
Safety Net? Y N If "Yes," then what safety net(s):_____	Safety Net? Y N If "Yes," then what safety net(s):_____	Safety Net? Y N If "Yes," then what safety net(s):_____	Safety Net? Y N If "Yes," then what safety net(s):_____

School Genetics: A Blueprint for Saving Public Schools

When Tier 1 support no longer worked, students would be offered support on the needs-based tier, or Tier 2. Supports are strategies that allow for interventions to take place. This includes time before, during, and after the school day that allow staff to work with students.

This is an appropriate point to discuss one of the key elements in school improvement. All students can indeed learn, but at different rates, and under different conditions. The most critical nonhuman factor in helping students learn is **TIME**. If given enough time, most students can find success in our classrooms. However, time is a rare commodity. The time students have with their teachers is shared among all of the students in the classrooms. When you add interruptions, disruptions to the learning environment, and other teacher responsibilities, that time is woefully cut. Therefore, one of the most important things a principal can do is develop a strong master schedule that allows for extra time to remediate and/or enrich students who need it. Before and after school programs are wonderful, but many students cannot get to school early or stay after school for a host of reasons. The best way to control student learning is during the school hours. Even a 20-minute-a-day remediation period over the course of 180-student day calendar equals 60 hours of added instructional support. That can surely be the difference between passing and failing a state standardized test. It could also be the difference in passing and exceeding on a state standardized test.

Interventions are the research-based practices that are used to treat student deficiencies. Interventions are used as long as needed to remedy the problem. An assessment is given after a few days of treatment and the intervention will be either completed, continued if needed, or discarded based upon effectiveness after testing.

At the Tier 2 level, assessments must occur more frequently than at the Tier 1 level. Students who receive Tier 2 level support receive all of the Tier 1 support, but they also get intensive support at other times during the school day. At this tier, we introduce more formalized progress monitoring. Progress monitoring is the practice of assessing student performance on an instructional task after academic interventions have been used. We recommend progress monitoring at least once a week for these students. Again, the academic coaches at TCUES orchestrated the Tier 2 program and tracked the data for these students. We enlisted the help of paraprofessionals and other staff members to aid in the Tier 2 support process since most teachers were either in their classrooms or on planning.

One pitfall that schools want to avoid is placing students in a tier and the child becoming trapped in that tier for the rest of his or her school career. To this end, we used decision-making tools to gauge when a student was ready to go from Tier 2 back to Tier 1 or if he or she should be elevated to Tier 3. These decisions were made once every nine weeks by the RtI team and with teacher consultation. On the next two pages are samples of decision-making forms.

School Genetics: A Blueprint for Saving Public Schools

Decision Making Form

Student's Name _____ Grade Level _____

Homeroom Teacher _____

	1st 9 Weeks			2nd 9 Weeks			3rd 9 Weeks			4th 9 Weeks		
	Tier			Tier			Tier			Tier		
	score		grade level −below √ at +above	score		grade level −below √ at +above	score		grade level −below √ at +above	score		grade level −below √ at +above
CRCT Math '07												
CRCT Rdg '07												
Math Benchmark (Quarterly)												
Rdg Benchmark (Quarterly)												
DRA (3 times per year)												
STAR Math (3 times per year)												
STAR Reading (3 times per year)												
STEEP (3 times per year)												
Math Navigator												

Taylor County Upper Elementary School
Teaching Children Effective Strategies for Success in Life

Page 1

School Genetics: A Blueprint for Saving Public Schools

1st 9 Weeks   *Date* _____

Team decision _____

Rationale _____

_____

2nd 9 Weeks   *Date* _____

Team decision _____

Rationale _____

_____

3rd 9 Weeks   *Date* _____

Team decision _____

Rationale _____

_____

4th 9 Weeks   *Date* _____

Team decision _____

Rationale _____

_____

Page 2

School Genetics: A Blueprint for Saving Public Schools

Tier 3 support was very similar to Tier 2 except that we increased the number of supports, interventions, and progress monitoring. Students who were placed at Tier 3 had not been successful in Tier 2 after a minimum of two different research-based interventions. Another key difference for these students is that only certified personnel with specialized training would conduct these interventions. In the case of TCUES, those people were the academic coaches. Tier 3 cases would involve the school's Student Support Team (SST) when needed to review progress. Before a student would be placed in the SST process, the RtI team had to approve the recommendation to move forward. Before we began this practice, any teacher could refer a student to the SST Coordinator at any time, thus leading to an abundance of uncoordinated referrals, an inordinate amount of paperwork and meetings, and a recommendation that had often been made through emotions and not much hard evidence. Our revised process helped with the cessation of over-identification of students going into the pipeline that leads to special education.

Tier 4 in Georgia refers to students with special needs--including students with learning/emotional disabilities, gifted students, and students who are English Language Learners. For the purpose of this discussion, I refer to learning and emotionally impaired special education students as students with disabilities, or SWD. The SWD population in the school was rather high, so we knew that we had to do two things: 1) reduce the number of students who were entering the SWD category, and 2) "do something" with students who were already in that category. Our former

SWD program was rather traditional and not well monitored. We began the process of co-teaching, a process in which a special education teacher was paired with a regular education teacher, and eligible SWD students received their on-grade level instruction with their peers. We saw tremendous success with this practice, and we expanded it throughout the school. SWD students were receiving all of the support of Tiers 1, 2, and 3, but were also receiving access to the general education curriculum by way of co-teaching. Their Individualized Education Plans were adapted to meet their specific needs and were not "cookie cutter" plans as had been seen in the past. Co-teaching is an acquired art form. Most teachers began their careers being the sage on the stage, and now that stage was to be shared. It requires teachers to move ego aside and cooperate with another person. This is a marriage in which the school leadership must take great care to pair the right two individuals together. There are even compatibility forms existing to aid schools in creating the right co-teaching teams. In an effective co-teaching team, an observer should not be able to tell the regular education teacher from the special education teacher. A strong pairing with proper guidance and support can do wonders for student achievement.

LESSON 7

NEWTON HIGH SCHOOL: RAMS RISE!

The practices used at Taylor Upper Elementary worked for them, but could they work at a high school with nearly 2000 students and 120 staff members? Well, the plan had to be bigger. More people were needed to coordinate efforts. A RtI team was in place, but it was more clearly differentiated from the Design Team. In fact, the two teams were not the same, but representatives served on both groups. The RtI process at NHS included academic coaches who oversaw Tier 1, a graduation coach who not only coordinated the entire program, but also directly oversaw Tiers 2 and 3, and a special education department chair who oversaw Tier 4. Please note that just as with TCUES, academic coaches and a graduation coach were people who did not have direct classroom responsibilities and could use their time to support the regular educational program. The RtI Coordinator led a team of RtI Managers who worked directly with students identified at Tiers 2 through 4. These RtI Managers were a group of 17 teachers who were given planning time to meet with their caseload of students and monitor their progress. The managers worked closely with teachers to inform them of needs that the students may have. The managers reported to the RtI Coordinator, who in turn worked with both the assistant principal and principal in analyzing data and making instructional adjustments.

School Genetics: A Blueprint for Saving Public Schools

The RtI Coordinator created a chart that allowed for us to see if students had academic needs and/or discipline needs. The sample is provided below:

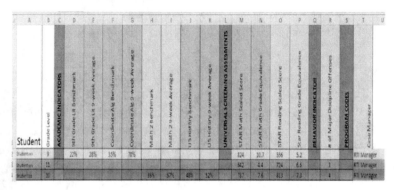

The chart highlights students that had academic issues, behavioral issues, and students that had both.

When you compare experiences at Taylor County Upper Elementary School and Newton High School, strong Response to Intervention programs have key components:

1. Staff who do not have direct classroom responsibilities can oversee processes. In both cases, academic and/or graduation coaches were essential. The academic coaches were compensated through federal funding support; so wise use of this funding is needed.
2. A master schedule that provided support time for students and common planning for teachers is critical.

School Genetics: A Blueprint for Saving Public Schools

When you compare experiences at Taylor County Upper Elementary School and Newton High School, strong Response to Intervention programs have key components:

1. Staff who do not have direct classroom responsibilities can oversee processes. In both cases, academic and/or graduation coaches were essential. The academic coaches were compensated through federal funding support; so wise use of this funding is needed.
2. A master schedule that provided support time for students and common planning for teachers is critical.
3. Research-based-interventions and a process for progress monitoring are needed to track student growth.
4. Implementation with fidelity is achieved through weekly meetings of the RtI Team. The team reviewed and refined practices by keeping a laser sharp focus on the needs of the students, teachers, and the school.

After placing the RtI program in effect at Newton High, the school saw academic gains within a short period of time. The chart on the following page shows how student achievement increased on eight state standardized tests students took in 2010-11 and 2011-12 school years.

School Genetics: A Blueprint for Saving Public Schools

Course	2010-2011 Pass	**2011-2012 pass**	% Pass rate Increased
9th Grade Lit	80	**88.3**	8.3
American Lit	84	**90.1**	6.1
Math I	39	**66.7**	27.7
Math II	36	**51.2**	15.2
Biology	61	**79**	18
US History	76	**78.32**	2.32
Physcial Science	77	**88.3**	11.3
Econ	70	**77.7**	7.7

LESSON 8

DISCIPLINE

Quality instruction begets quality discipline. If teaching and learning are occurring at a high rate, there is little time for disciplinary issues to occur. At the same time, without discipline, there cannot be teaching and learning. Discipline and instruction are cycles that go hand-in-hand.

Every person loves and believes in discipline in schools. Discipline is the "**gene**" in school **genetics**. I have had parents ask to tour the school before enrolling their children. They were not always there to observe the rigor of instruction, but they wanted to observe the climate and the events and actions taking place in the building. They wanted to make sure their children would be safe. Parents send their children to school with the expectation that their children will return home to them the exact same way they left with the exception that the student is a little more educated than the day before. When parents and communities feel that discipline is not a priority in schools, then trust in the school fades. Let's go back to the discussion of what a good school is. When I ask the question, "What is a good school?" I often get camouflaged answers. The answer usually begins with order, which means that discipline is in place. People want their children to be safe. I have three school-age children at the time of this writing, and I want them to be safe at school. The thought of another child deliberately deciding to target and hurt my children is an abomination; *these are my children*! If you ever want to get a person "fighting mad," tamper with her money, food, and/or children. Our children bring forth our protective instinct and a passion in us that we will lay down our very lives for. I would gamble to say most parents feel this way. With such feelings, it is fully understandable that parents want their children to be safe at school. Some schools, although they are not the best schools when compared to others in test scores, are still revered by community members because they are safe and orderly. At the end of the day, some parents care more about safety than they do the academic achievement of the school itself. Academic achievement can be obtained through the support of the parents at home, but safety at school is something parents have very limited control over. Discipline is one of the major reasons some parents choose to leave public education and pursue alternative means of educating their children.

Discipline and order in schools are a basic right and necessity. When you study Maslow's Hierarchy of Needs, safety is one the most basic needs a person must have in order to reach more complex levels of learning and success. No child can concentrate on academics when she is scared. A fight in a classroom is so disruptive that even the best teachers struggle with regaining order after the event. Order and structure are necessary for learning to take place.

Classroom management is a topic that is taught to varying degrees by colleges and other educational agencies. The focus has remained on improving academics, specifically reading and mathematics. Federal funding has focused mostly on improving academics, and behavioral problems are usually financed locally, if at all. While media outlets publicize egregious behaviors regularly, politicians and the general public seem to focus discussion on academic achievement failures that malign many schools. Educators fully realize, however, that if there is to be achievement, there must first be order. Disruptive behavior in classrooms reduces the amount of quality instructional time. Student suspensions and expulsions also reduce time students are in classes learning. Bullying distracts victims to the point that learning is nearly impossible. The effect of these and other disciplinary issues are cumulative in nature, and it leads to instructional time lost. Time lost is achievement lost. To improve instructional time-on-task, discipline must be structured, and classroom management must be effective.

The discipline issues seen in schools can be horrendous. Schools have been plagued with student discipline issues for decades (and longer), but our current American culture tends to define educators as lesser professionals while at the same time glorifying poor behavior. Teaching was once a time-honored profession in which teachers were respected. Today, teachers are cursed, disrespected, and even assaulted by the very children they choose to protect and teach. Many parents also exhibit these same behaviors to teachers and administrators. I have personally been stabbed in the hand with a pair of scissors while breaking up a student fight. A close colleague of mine had his eye socket broken, and another had his nose broken; both were trying to stop student fights. I know many teachers who have been injured in attempts to calm student melees and outbursts. I have seen teachers' faces scratched from top to bottom. A teacher friend of mine was nearly blinded when a contact cracked in his eye while trying to stop a fight. I have seen countless pushes, scratches, and injuries caused by unruly students. That does not include classroom destruction of both school and personal property. On top of that, I know of many teachers who have had personal belongings stolen with no recourse. The list of atrocities teachers and school employees could tell is endless. The teachers and school employees who have been physically and emotionally hurt have families, husbands, wives, children, and others who care about them. Now, sharing this information alone does not improve schools. I share it because I rarely hear non-educators talking about the plight of the contemporary American school teacher. The media has not taken a stance to show the world how difficult and in fact dangerous teaching can be for educators. News media rarely, if ever, tells the stories of those who have been hurt in the line of duty. The story never focuses on how the teacher was hurt; if anything, it focuses on how the teacher did something wrong that led to the problem. The teacher's story is rarely told publicly. Because of this lopsided version of justice, many teachers have given up; you cannot teach in a hostile environment. They burnout and lose the passion that made them choose this field in the first place. Many teachers leave the profession because, quite frankly, they do not feel safe or do not feel supported by administration when issues arise. You would be surprised at how many teachers can be found crying in the parking lot as they get ready to enter their schools. In these school environments, the students are in control of the culture, thus making the school genetically undesirable for effective teaching and learning to take place.

Student-to-student issues are just as bad. Thanks to the introduction of cell phone cameras and social media, student fights can be seen instantly at any time. Bullying has evolved into cyberbullying, and students are not the only targets of these bullies.

Bullying: The Elusively Real Epidemic

Let's take a moment to explore the bullying issue a bit further. We justifiably view this problem as an epidemic that is destroying our schools from the inside out. If one were to delve deeply into most disciplinary issues, bullying is often an element of the problem.

There are several aspects of bullying that we do not address properly, and that may be why we cannot seem to get a handle on this problem. First, bullying has existed since the dawn of human civilization. By nature, there have always been humans who seek to intimidate, dominate, or threaten others they perceive to be weaker than them for their own reasons. Slavery can be described as the most prolific use of bullying that has ever existed. Virtually every adult today has either been bullied, was a bully, or has witnessed bullying. This is not new. I was bullied as a child, and one of my children was the target of bullies for several years. Children have taken their own lives and the lives of others because of the crippling effects of bullying. This is a painful ordeal that no family should have to endure. Our current societal views and culture have taken a problem that has always existed and made it a mainstream issue in which everyone wants justice, but the path to success is not clearly established. The problem is that the solution is still not readily available to address the epidemic, and schools normally take the blame for this.

What Bullying Is (And Is Not)

Reality check: schools are not equipped to address bullying to the fullest extent possible. First, the term "bullying" means different things to different people. Typically, bullying must have these three elements present to be clearly described as bullying:

1. Must be a pattern--there is a difference between bullying and student conflict. Student conflicts are random and isolated. If a situation occurs in which the same aggressor instigates an attack on the same victim two or more times, then it is more likely that bullying can be proven.

2. Must be targeted--The aggressor must attack a specific person or persons and focuses on that individual(s). This proves that the acts are not by chance but are deliberate in nature.

3. Must be one-sided--A clear pattern of targeted aggression towards a victim must be established. Often, school

administrators investigate bullying issues and find that both parties play a role in the dispute. This is a rivalry, not necessarily bullying. A rivalry may stem from bullying, but once it has evolved into a rivalry, both parties end up sharing the blame, and often times, the consequences. When consequences are given in these situations, the person who is usually blamed the most ends up not being the student who started the incident, but unfortunately, the school administrator.

Point number three leads to the biggest problem with addressing bullying: it is normally an invisible crime. Adults rarely see bullying take place, and schools often have to take one student's word versus another. Unless there is physical evidence, video surveillance, or a confession from the bully, these cases are hard to prove. For the record, bullies rarely confess or self-identify, and they often have friends who cover for them. Administrators are usually taking a stab in the dark when trying to investigate these claims, and the evidence is typically scant. Worst of all, the parents of the alleged bully often take great offense at their child being labeled a bully, and this leads to greater conflict that usually distract schools from the root problem. In all of this, the victim gets lost in the shuffle.

The problem has been further compounded thanks to social media. Videos of fights and other inappropriate behaviors can be found and shared with the world instantly. Sexting and profane, threatening texts run rampant among our youth. While this happens, our government has yet to take definitive steps that could curb such behavior. By not acting, we are condoning this deplorable behavior. Even though social media allows for us to obtain hard evidence of bullying, our current laws still leave much room for perpetrators to get away with the act if the transmission occurs on private property before or after school hours. Cyberbullying, like bullying, is terroristic in nature. The government has yet to take aggressive action against inappropriate comments, videos, and blogs largely due to the fact that the perpetrators of these acts can hide behind cowardly anonymous disguises and feel privileged to abuse free speech rights. Until the government takes decisive action to curtail cyberbullying, we will continue to slip into social decay and our country will suffer.

The Need for Supportive Parenting

Parents play a critical role in improving school climate. There was a time when, if you asked parents what they wanted out of school for their children, the answer would be "to get an education." Many parents' behaviors say that the thing they want most out of school is for their children "to be happy." This happiness equates to "let the child do whatever he wants to do without regard to rules." Too many parents, in displaced love, make excuses for their children and defend wrongdoing. This is a national problem that leads to a "softening" of the next generation. Children need to learn how to struggle and survive independent of their parents. They need to learn how to make mistakes and fix them without parents swooping in to save them. By coddling our children, we are not equipping them to compete with their counterparts around the world. We tie the hands of school administrators and teachers by carrying out the same demeaning, disrespectful behaviors that the children exhibit. Again, the school system is a microcosm of the community. If the community is suffering, the children in the schools are suffering. As parents, we must stop enabling our children and hold them accountable for high expectations both academically and socially. This is not solely the responsibility of the schools; in fact, this is mostly the responsibility of the home.

What is even more maddening about these problems is that our country is not willing to end this trend. First, virtually no direct state or federal funding is funneled into schools to address the social and emotional disorders that affect our students. Grants are available, but are often time-limited and come with too many restrictions. Students of all economic conditions need a system of support that includes social workers, therapeutic counselors, mental health therapists, and psychologists at their disposal in every school. A school resource officer should be in all schools. In some communities, gang violence is prevalent; in others, school shootings reign. The violence is not limited to race. Yet, we have not come together as a country to place resources in every school to safeguard our students and employees.

Secondly, our federal special education laws (known as IDEA), which were created to make sure that all children received fair and equitable treatment so that the playing field for education was leveled, has been perverted, abused, and corrupted by unscrupulous attorneys, "advocates," and parents who use protective rules of IDEA to uphold inappropriate behavior by students with special needs. IDEA was meant to give students who need support a fair chance to get an education, but it is too often used to justify inappropriate behaviors. I have witnessed students classified as having special needs brutalize other students, but their "advocates" manipulate the situation so that the special needs student becomes the "victim," and the true victims are lost in the battle. This mentality has led to many students feeling that they are in control of their school settings.

A close pastor and friend of mine once said, "The teachers are afraid of the administrators. The administrators are afraid of the parents. The parents are afraid of the students. And the students ain't afraid of anybody!" There was a time when adults were united in raising children. Today many parents often blame the school for any disciplinary issues that occur with their children, which serve as a distraction from the real problem. This model is backwards and the best way to annihilate public schools.

Thirdly, our country as a whole appears to have lost its value system in regards to education. While discipline problems have always existed, there was a time when the village was truly allowed to raise a child. There was also a time when children were seen and not heard. America is a wealthy country with a lot of excess, and we give our children this excess. We are hard workers, but other developing countries work harder because they still struggle to be better. This struggle makes education a commodity in these countries. In the United States, we are taking education for granted. Thanks to our Constitution, education for us is not a privilege, but an entitled right. Thus, teachers and schools are taken for granted. The culture of our students is driven by the Internet, television, and music, not by our homes, schools, and churches. Where parents used to uphold the school in disciplinary issues, many parents now blame the school, teachers, and/or principals for any problems that arise with their children. I have served as an administrator for fourteen years as of this writing, yet I have personally witnessed only a very small percentage of parents apologize for their child's actions or admit guilt. As I said before, every person loves and believes in discipline in schools. That is, until the discipline involves their child. Many unfortunate administrators now believe that the fight after administering discipline to a student can become so time consuming, arduous, and even career threatening that it is best to ignore the matter. Again, a vicious cycle of apathy, and ill-placed student entitlement persists that distracts us from the true goal: providing a quality education.

The dilemma that many people outside of public education do not understand is that this business is not like any other business. The product we produce is human. Humans possess free will and independent thought, and no manual or written procedures can always fix these issues. Public education has rules that do not make education as easy as one would think. For example, there are compulsory attendance laws in which public schools must constitutionally educate all of its students. Even though some students choose to reject formal education as evidenced by their behaviors, but they are obligated to attend until a certain age. Many private schools can easily remove unruly students, but students in public schools have due process rights. Special education students have even more protections that often enable poor behavior and give them a form of "diplomatic immunity" that forgives even the most egregious behaviors. Basically, the public school system has to find ways to provide education to students in spite of themselves.

It is my hope that the previous section sparks meaningful conversation and subsequent action to right these wrongs. Federal funds need to be given to school districts to hire staff that can aid in dealing with the mental and emotional needs that our children have. Schools do hold a great deal of responsibility in the reforming and educating of children, but this must be done in partnership with parents and the community. The home is the first teacher, and parents must be held accountable for the behavior that children exhibit in school. What may appear to be tough love now may serve to create a productive citizen in the future. In fact, tough, structured love is needed to effectively grow children into contributing members of society. I firmly believe that all children are entitled to a free and appropriate education. The key word is "appropriate." Every child should have the right to an education, but a child's education should not be provided in a regular teaching environment when it is clearly so disruptive that this education comes at the expense of other children who genuinely go to school to learn. The time has come for us to reclaim education and bring it back to a place of esteem and value.

School Genetics: A Blueprint for Saving Public Schools

What Works in School Discipline

Despite the gloom and doom of the previous section, all hope is not lost. When teachers create very clear rules, rituals, and routines, students thrive. All teachers and the school administrators must be reasonably consistent with the establishing of these rules. Also, egregious behaviors cannot be tolerated. This is sometimes tough, but consistency and fairness will transform a school. While at Taylor County Upper Elementary, we began to address discipline issues in the same manner as we addressed academic issues. Below is discipline pyramid of intervention chart we created:

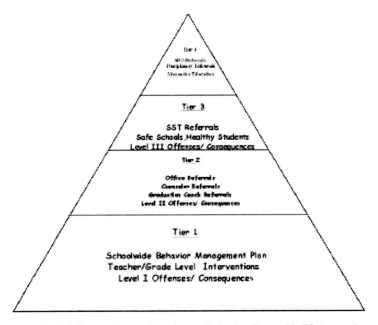

Taylor County Upper Elementary Behavior Pyramid of Interventions

School Genetics: A Blueprint for Saving Public Schools

At TCUES, the discipline committee analyzed discipline data and identified Tiers 2 through 4 students every nine weeks. The academic tiers of these students were compared with their behavioral tiers. Interventions were then selected based upon the information that was learned. Based on the referral system below, we were pretty effective with curbing many undesired behaviors:

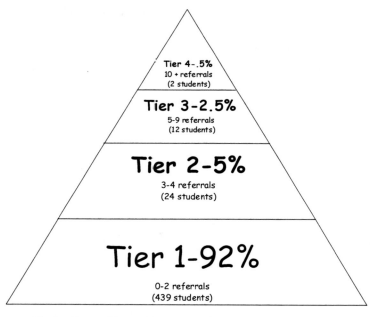

Taylor County Upper Elementary Behavior Statistics Fall 2008

Positive Behavior Interventions and Supports (PBIS)

Discipline issues at elementary schools are, in most cases, a lot different than their high school counterparts. High school is a different animal altogether. Whereas TCUES was

School Genetics: A Blueprint for Saving Public Schools

an elementary school with 600 young children, Newton High School was a school with over 1,800 high school students, many of whom not only had the typical rebellious teenage attitude, but were also the victims of generational poverty and a world full of technological stimulation. To combat this type of scenario, we used Positive Behavior Interventions and Supports (PBIS) extensively. PBIS, when implemented effectively, can reduce the number of disciplinary infractions and promote a more positive school climate. PBIS focuses on positive reinforcement or key rules that embody a school. As the principal of Newton High School, I led the implementation of this process with the support of the district office and Georgia Department of Education.

To make Newton High better, we adopted the best practices taught through Positive Behavior Interventions and Supports. Instead of focusing totally on consequences for negative behavior, we began to shift the focus to acknowledging positive behavior. There is usually more "behaving" going on in schools instead of "misbehaving. Misbehavior is so sensationalized that it captures our attention, while most students are passively doing as they are told. PBIS gives a voice to the voiceless.

The first thing that had to be done was to create a PBIS Team of teachers who would make sure the work got done. This is critical. Many initiatives fail when there is not the appropriate staff dedicated and supported to seeing the project through to completion. The PBIS team was charged with developing a highly functional program, and this team was given tremendous authority and flexibility by the Principal. The Principal is the Gatekeeper at the school; what he promotes (or not) is what gets done. The original PBIS team at NHS included teachers from all departments so that the entire faculty had a voice.

Next, the school had to develop expectations for acceptable behaviors at Newton High. Newton High's mascot is the Rams, so we created a slogan that embodied the word, "RAMS":

We are Rams!
We Are Respectful!
We Are Accountable!
We Are Motivated!
We Are Successful!
We Are Rams!
Rams, Rise!

School Genetics: A Blueprint for Saving Public Schools

Once we created these expectations, we had to describe to students exactly what those expectations looked like in various areas of the school including classrooms, hallways, bathrooms, the cafeteria, and the media center. We created posters to remind students of what was to be expected in the school.

WE ARE **RAMS**

	Hallways	Commons	Restrooms	Cafeteria
Respectful	I will use appropriate language. I will keep school property clean.	I will be courteous to others. I will use appropriate language.	I will keep the restrooms clean.	I will be courteous. I will wait my turn. I will use appropriate language.
Accountable	I will be in class when the bell rings. I will use the proper pass system.	I will avoid negative situations. I will only use vending machines during the appropriate times.	I will flush. I will place trash in the trash can.	I will throw away my tray. I will place trash in the trash can.
Motivated	I will be prepared for class. I will walk with a purpose. Keep Clean: I will pick up trash even though it is not mine.	I will move with a purpose (keep it moving).	P2- I will potty with a purpose. I will report any problems to a teacher.	I will eat with a purpose. Keep Clean: I will pick up trash even though it is not mine.
Successful	I will dress appropriately.	I will be aware of my surroundings.	I will clean up after myself.	I will leave the area better than I found it. I will return to class on time.

The next step was to describe the traits that a Newton High School student should exhibit. The ideal Newton High School students should, upon graduation, possess a certain level of marketable skills. Our original thoughts changed from a sketch to a model poster that was placed in the school.

School Genetics: A Blueprint for Saving Public Schools

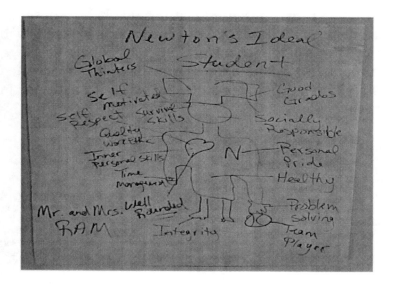

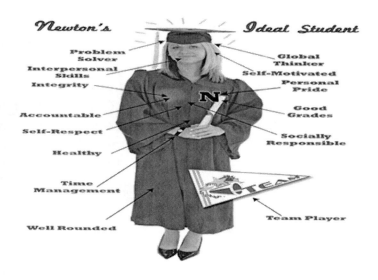

School Genetics: A Blueprint for Saving Public Schools

Another issue we had to address was the use of common language among teachers. Inconsistency among teachers gives students loopholes that they use to get way with inappropriate behaviors. For example, "tardy to class" means one thing to Teacher A and something else to Teacher B. We called the common non-negotiable language our " universals." All teachers and students were taught what an acceptable practice for universal was and the PBIS team was the group that made these determinations with input from the staff.

Another part of establishing a common language for behaviors is helping staff see what offenses should be handled in the classroom and what should be referred to the office. Criminal activity, chronic misbehaviors, severe disruptions to learning, and disrespect to teachers/staff should be sent to the office, and minor offenses should be dealt with progressively in the classroom. Teachers must be careful to never give away their power to other adults because children know when you are not able to handle them. I used to tell my staff, "There are misdemeanors, felonies, disasters, and apocalyptic events. You handle the misdemeanors, and the administration will handle the felonies. I handle disasters. If it is an apocalyptic event, then we call the central office." In other words, address problems at the appropriate levels so that proper and effective consequences can be administered.

One way in which students and staff were acknowledged was through incentive programs. Pictures of some of the ideas we implemented are shown on the next page.

School Genetics: A Blueprint for Saving Public Schools

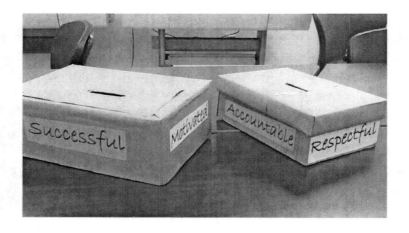

School Genetics: A Blueprint for Saving Public Schools

One of the most successful components of the Newton High PBIS program was the creation of a student-led version of the PBIS team, the Rambassadors. The Rambassadors was the first recognized group of its type according to the Georgia State Department of Education. This group of students comes from all grades and behavior backgrounds. They are scholars, athletes, artists, and everything in between. They were interviewed to become the student ambassadors of the school. Known as leaders amongst their peers, the Rambassadors support students and encourage positive behaviors from their classmates.

Did any of this work? Although there is still much to be done, the graph on the following page depicts how PBIS impacted school climate after one semester of implementation.

School Genetics: A Blueprint for Saving Public Schools

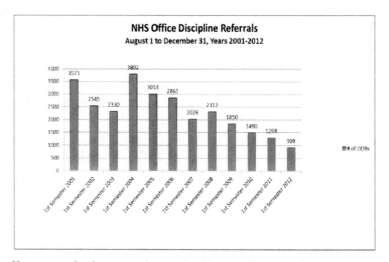

As illustrated, the number of office referrals for NHS students during that first semester was the lowest since 2001. The demographics of the school had changed, but the behaviors had improved. Perhaps the biggest force that led to this change is that we were able to actually reach the hearts of the students. They chose to rise up and perform better. The culture had changed, and learning could effectively take place.

CONCLUSION

School Improvement is not an exact science, but certain best practices were common in both Taylor County Upper Elementary and Newton High School that led to success. When implemented with fidelity the following practices keep the school on the right track: professional learning teams that meet weekly, a focus on the right work, and the supports to get the work done. In the case of Taylor County Upper Elementary, the school moved from being in Needs Improvement year Six to becoming a Title I Distinguished School in 2009. Taylor County Upper Elementary School was also in the inaugural class of the Student Support Team Association of Georgia Educators (SSTAGE) for receiving the SSTAGE Star Award for Promising Practices, Elementary Division, in 2009.

Newton High School was in its first year of Needs Improvement in 2010. By using the aforementioned practices, the school was named a Title I Reward School not only in 2012, but in 2013 as well. Like Taylor County Upper Elementary, Newton High School received the SSTAGE Star Award for Promising Practices, High School Division, in 2014.

In addition, Newton High School was named a High Flying School, which is an award given to only five schools in the nation annually that possess high poverty and high achievement rates. From 2011 to the time of this writing, the graduating of Newton High earned over $37 million in scholarships. Newton High also received state recognition for its Response to Intervention implementation.

You cannot change your genetics, but you can enhance genetic traits. Just as diet and exercises can increase healthier living and a better body, focused work on teaching, learning, and discipline can improve schools. The beautiful thing about school improvement is that it is contagious. When people see success, then they want to join that team. Success begets success. It takes compassion, commitment, and extreme focus. There is not time for distractions and even less time for excuses. Although cliché, the statement is true: Our kids can't wait for us to get this right.

The time has come for a genetic study. What is your school's genetic makeup? Are you honest with yourself? Do you truly want change, and are you committed to seeing it occur? The resources to improve your school are at your disposal. Public education is the greatest treasure of any society. Let's show our constituents that we have the tools and skills necessary to enhance the genetic code of our schools for the betterment of our communities.

REFERENCES

DuFour, R., DuFour, R., Eaker, R., & Karhanek, G. (2004). *Whatever It Takes*. Bloomington: Solution Tree.

Dweck, C. (2006). *Mindset: The New Psychology of Success*. New York: Ballantine Books.

Kliebard, H. (1995). The Curriculum of the Dewey School. In *The Struggle for the American Curriculum* (2nd ed.). New York: Routledge.

Marzano, R. (2004). *Building Background Knowledge*. Alexandria: ASCD.

Marzano, R., Pickering, D., & Pollock, J. (2001). *Classroom Instruction That Works: Research-Based Strategies for Increasing Student Achievement*. Alexandria: ASCD.

Payne, R. (2005). *A Framework for Understanding Poverty* (4th ed.). Highlands: Aha! Process.

CPSIA information can be obtained at www.ICGtesting.com
Printed in the USA
LVOW10s1028140915

453994LV00028BA/887/P